MONEY
Money
MONEY

Where It Comes From
How to Save It
Spend It ✺ Make It

EVE DROBOT

ILLUSTRATED BY
CLAUDIA DÁVILA

MAPLE
TREE
PRESS

Maple Tree Press Inc.

51 Front Street East, Suite 200, Toronto, Ontario M5E 1B3

www.mapletreepress.com

Distributed in Canada by Raincoast Books
9050 Shaughnessy Street, Vancouver, British Columbia V6P 6E5

Distributed in the United States by Publishers Group West
1700 Fourth Street, Berkeley, California 94710

We acknowledge the financial support of the Canada Council for the Arts, the Ontario Arts
Council, the Government of Canada through the Book Publishing Industry Development
Program (BPIDP), and the Government of Ontario through the Ontario Media Development
Corporation's Book Initiative for our publishing activities.

Cataloguing in Publication Data

Drobot, Eve, 1951-

Money, money, money : where it comes from, how to save it, spend it and make it /
written by Eve Drobot ; illustrated by Claudia Dávila.

Includes index.

ISBN 1-897066-10-4 (bound).   ISBN 1-897066-11-2 (pbk.)

1. Money—Juvenile literature. I. Dávila, Claudia II. Drobot, Eve, 1951- . Money. III. Title.

HG221.5.D76 2004   j332.4   C2004-902676-3

Design & art direction: Claudia Dávila
Illustrations: Claudia Dávila

Printed in China

A   B   C   D   E   F

CONTENTS

Money, Money, Money!

Pick a coin or a bill out of your pocket and look at it as though you've never seen one before. There are all sorts of distinguishing marks and features on money: portraits of famous people, images of some sort—often a flower or an animal—words and numbers that tell you how much the piece is worth and when it was made, even security features. Each element that makes up a coin or a bill serves a purpose and has a story behind it.

What you probably know most about money is how to spend it. How much money you have to spend on trading cards, going to the movies, or buying a pair of funky striped socks at the mall depends on many things. Your mom or dad—or both—earns money at a job, and out of that money has to pay for the roof over your head, the food on your table, the clothes you wear, and other things you don't see, like taxes or insurance. And out of that comes the money you get, whether as a bit here and there as you need it, or the specific amount that is your allowance.

In North America, many kids can count on a weekly allowance; the amount depends on the financial circumstances of each family. Some parents hand an allowance over with no strings attached. Others give it in exchange for chores done around the house. In some parts of the world, kids also get gifts of money on certain holidays, like Chinese New Year, or for their own special days, like a birthday, a bar mitzvah, or a graduation. But one thing seems universal: money—making it, saving it, and spending it—is a subject of interest the world over.

JAR STAR

What's the best way to handle money? Do you spend it? Save it? Give it away? You could do all three. Whether it's a gift, your allowance, or money you've earned from jobs like babysitting or shoveling snow, why not use the Three Jars to figure out how to manage your money?

Jar #1: The money you want to spend now—okay, so it doesn't stay in the jar very long.

Jar #2: The money you want to save until you have enough for a special purchase, like a computer game or tickets to a theme park for a day with your friends.

Jar #3: The money you give away. Whoa! *Give away?* One of the joys of having money is knowing you can share it with those less fortunate than you, through your community, or a charitable organization that works for a cause you feel is important.

What Is Money?

Money comes in different shapes. Most of the people in the world use either bills or coins, stamped and marked by governments to say what each piece is worth. But until recently, in some faraway places such as the South Pacific or parts of Africa, you could use shells or beads. The Yap Islanders in the Pacific still trade great big stones with holes in the middle. The stones weigh as much as a compact car—not exactly the sort of money that would fit in a wallet.

If you think about it, money is really an idea, not a thing. Anything can be used as money as long as everyone agrees it is money. If you want a comic book your friend has and he accepts three pieces of bubble gum for it, then for that moment, bubble gum is money and one comic book is worth three pieces.

In the very early days, people didn't have money because no one had thought of it yet. They would exchange things for other things. One person would swap a cow, say, for a bag of potatoes and a big pot to cook them in. This system, called barter, worked quite well, and in some parts of the world it still does.

But what if you had a pot and potatoes that someone wanted, and you didn't need a cow right now? The person could say, "I'll take your pot and potatoes now. When you want my cow, you can get it from me." But will she keep her word? You'd feel better if she gave you something that stood for the cow, a symbol or a token of her promise.

Then if everyone agreed on what that token should be, you wouldn't even have to trade it in for the cow. You could give it to a third person in exchange for a blanket, and he could bring the token to the first person and take the cow. The token is what we now call money.

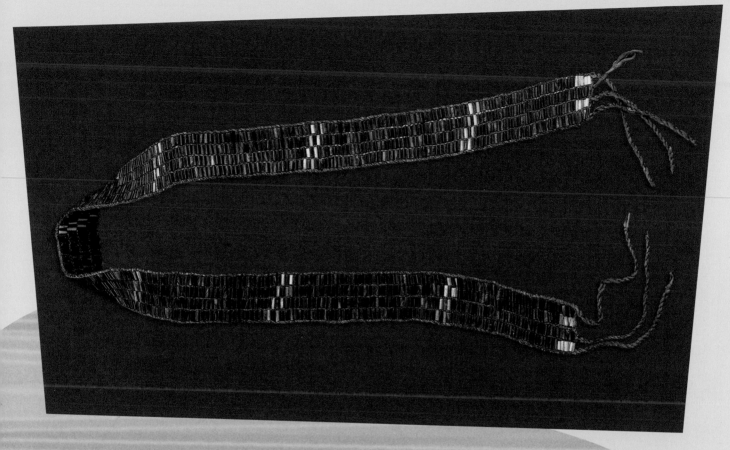

SHELLING IT OUT

Wampum (above) means "white" in the language of the Algonkian Native people of North America. It was what they called the polished and cut periwinkle and clam shells that they bartered for many things. Each tribe had its own designs for stringing the shells together and used them to decorate belts, capes, shoes, and earrings. The Iroquois have used the highly valued wampum as prizes in sports, for marriage proposals, to honor important people, to pay for a crime, to maintain peace, and to ransom hostages.

CHECK it out!

Money has gone a long way from being a symbol for a cow or a blanket or a pot. When you hold a coin or a bank note in your hand, you have no way of knowing what it's really worth. But you do know it will buy you what you want. It's a matter of trust.

CHAPTER 1

THE HISTORY OF

MONEY

From Beans to Bills

efore coins and bills came to be, early people in different places used all kinds of different materials and methods as their tokens for trade. Usually they chose something rare or valuable. In ancient Ethiopia, where salt was precious, blocks of salt could be traded for anything. More than 4,000 years ago, the Chinese, who valued fine metal tools, made miniature copper spades, knives, swords, and hoes as symbols of the real things to use as money.

In other places, the token wasn't necessarily a rare thing, just something everyone agreed on—stones and beads in Africa, whales' teeth in Fiji, and even bird feathers in the other South Pacific islands of Vanuatu. In ancient Tibet, people pressed tea leaves very tightly together into thin bricks stamped with designs, which they used for trading. The Aztecs, the ancient people of Mexico, had lots of cocoa beans around, so they used them as coins because they didn't see any other use for them. Then someone discovered you could make chocolate from cocoa beans.

When most people were farmers, livestock was their most important currency. In the lands of the Bible and in Africa, wealth was measured according to how many cattle, sheep, or goats a person had. In the country now known as Sri Lanka, big money was really big: it was elephants.

Lydian coins were the first coins. They were little bean-shaped pellets of gold mixed with silver—a metal known as "electrum"—and stamped to show their worth.

As Good As Gold

Over time, all over the world, metal proved to be the best thing for trading. Gold was especially popular because it was pretty, it didn't lose its shine, it was easy to shape into objects and—most important —it was rare. Gold rings were used as money in Egypt almost 6,000 years ago. Around the Aegean Sea, copper was preferred, and in Britain they used iron.

The problem was deciding how much gold, silver, copper, or iron to give for a cow or a blanket. Different countries had different ways of measuring

value, most of them based on weight. To do their business, storekeepers always used a scale to weigh the amount of metal being offered for their goods.

Then, more than 2,000 years ago, in the kingdom of Lydia (in what is now the nation of Turkey) the government started a new system. They made electrum coins, and marked them with an image to tell people how much each piece weighed and how pure it was. Now they could tell what the coin was worth just by looking at the stamp on it.

Alexander the Great's money was used throughout his empire, from Russia to the countries around the Nile, and from Greece to India.

Mug Shots

As coins became the standard form of money in the ancient world, the pictures stamped on them became more intricate. Local gods and goddesses appeared on coins; so did great military victories. Alexander the Great took over his father's throne in northern Greece in 336 B.C. He put his name and picture on a coin, and started a fad for rulers' portraits on money that has lasted to this day.

money myth

The legendary Greek hero Jason killed a dragon to steal the Golden Fleece, a sheepskin of pure gold. Could the Golden Fleece have been real? When the Greeks searched for gold in rivers, they dragged a sheepskin through the water to catch gold nuggets in its long hair. A sheepskin covered in gold nuggets might be the origin of the myth of the Golden Fleece.

Go for the Gold

The search for gold to make more coins was a constant one. The Spanish explorers landed in Mexico hoping to find spices to trade. When they saw how much gold the Aztecs had, they slaughtered 50,000 Natives in their greed for treasure. In 1533 the explorer Pizarro stole 13 tons of gold jewelry, statues, and religious artifacts from the Incas of Peru. He had everything melted down into ingots so he could carry it all back to Spain, and the beauty of each item was gone forever.

In 1849 the greatest gold rush in history took place in what is now California. In two years, 40,000 gold diggers unearthed 2.5 million ounces (over 70 million grams) of gold! Over the next ten years, they found ten times more. With the discovery of the Comstock Lode in Nevada in 1859, and the Klondike Rush to Alaska and the Yukon in 1896, gold prospectors flocked to the North American frontier.

One Australian who had gone to dig for gold in California in 1849 had no luck and decided to leave. But he didn't give up looking for gold when he got back home. In 1851 he struck it rich. When news spread, thousands upon thousands of people sailed immediately to Australia, hoping their luck would pan out too. The population of the country Down Under went from 400,000 to more than a million in only ten years.

Whether they were digging for gold, or sifting the rivers with pans (panning) for the precious nuggets, many gold prospectors settled in the American West and northern Canada after the gold rush ended.

11

Money You Can Fold

More than 2,000 years before the western world went off to dig for gold, the Chinese had already figured out a better system for doing business. Why bother unearthing metal when you can simply make money? That's what they did, printing it on an invention of theirs called paper.

About 600 years ago, the famous Italian adventurer Marco Polo visited the court of the Chinese emperor Kublai Khan. Marco Polo was amazed at what he saw, and brought stories back to Europe.

Money-back Guarantee

In the early years, paper money was quite simple. The bill was considered a promise to pay the person who had it the equivalent in gold or silver or in goods such as wool or tobacco. Soon, all the world's major paper currencies were "backed" by gold or silver, meaning that each dollar bill, pound note, mark, or franc was worth a certain amount of the precious metals. You could take your piece of paper to a bank and trade it in for silver or gold.

Over time, the paper notes themselves came to be considered valuable, and people began to trade them without regard to what they stood for. Today's five-dollar bill won't get you five dollar's worth of gold at a bank any more, but it will buy you five dollar's worth of ice cream at the store.

Marco Polo described in the accounts of his journey to China how each paper "coin" was cut, how much it was worth, and how each batch was stamped with the emperor's seal. "When thus coined in large quantities," Marco Polo wrote, "this paper currency is circulated in every part of the great Khan's dominions."

Socking It Away

When the English who had settled as colonists in America decided to become their own country, they fought a war against the British called the American Revolution. The colonial soldiers needed money, of course. But in the cold winter that their leader, General George Washington, and his men spent at Valley Forge, in Pennsylvania, they needed warmth even more.

So they took the paper money they were paid and, figuring there was nothing to spend it on right there and then, they stuffed it down their pants and into their socks for extra protection against the ice and snow. You could say this money was made into the first leg-warmers. The soldiers called their invention "shinplasters" because the bank notes were padded onto their shins.

Soldiers coined the term shinplasters, which has been used ever after to mean a bill or a bank note that isn't worth very much.

VALLEY FORGE   1778

No one had to tell *HIM* to save food & equipment

SAVE

ALL FOR ONE

Even though the Europeans heard about paper money from Marco Polo, they didn't start making their own until many centuries later. About 300 years ago, the government of Sweden ran out of silver, so it minted coins made of copper, which were worth much less. Swedes had to carry around heavy loads of copper coins, until the king gave permission to open a bank. The bank issued paper notes saying customers had a certain amount of coins there, and customers traded these notes, rather than the coins they represented.

Over centuries, European countries developed their own currencies: the French franc, the German mark, the Italian lira, and the Dutch florin, among others. As the countries became more linked with each other, the idea was born to have one kind of money for the continent. On January 1, 2002, twelve European countries began using the *euro*.

CHAPTER 2

MONEY

TALKS

What It's Called from A to Z

he word "money" comes from Latin, the language of the ancient Romans. Juno, one of their goddesses, was nicknamed Moneta, which means "the woman who warns." Juno was called that because one of her jobs was to warn people when they were doing wrong. She was an important goddess, and her temple was an important place. So it's not surprising that the ancient Romans made their coins right next to her temple. The coins themselves soon came to be called by the goddess's nickname.

Moneta is the word modern Italians still use to describe their coins. The Spanish call theirs *moneda* and the French say *monnaie*. The place where coins are made is called a "mint."

The first coins weren't all round—some were shaped like pie wedges. The Latin word for wedge, *cuneus*, gives us the English word "coin." But even though they had coins, the early Romans, like many ancient people, counted their wealth in how many cows they owned. Each head of cattle was called a *caput*, the Latin word for head. So if you had many cattle, you had lots of "capital"—a word we still use today to describe a pile of money.

Money Spoken Here

Many countries share the same name for their currency even if the money itself is different. Fourteen former colonies of France in Central Africa—from Benin to Togo—still use the French word *franc* even though France itself now calls its money *euros*.

Ten former colonies of Spain, including Cuba, Mexico, and Columbia, hang in with *peso*. England, although it is part of the European Community, hasn't gone euro and sticks with the *pound*, as do Lebanon, Malta, Sudan, and Egypt—perhaps to remind themselves of the old days when a bank note could be exchanged for one pound of silver. Denmark and Norway use the *krone*; Sweden and Iceland both flip their *kronas*, and the Czech Republic and Slovakia save their *korunas*—all words that mean "crown," because the money was once guaranteed by a king.

Money may be a common language around the globe, but the look of money is different the world over.

Seeing Dollar Signs

The dollar is known from Australia to Zimbabwe, in 23 countries in all. The word "dollar" originally comes from the German word *thaler*. When a German emperor became the king of Spain in the 17th century, Spanish explorers and conquerors took the German word to the Americas, and from there it kept going until it reached all around the world.

No one is absolutely sure where the $ sign came from, but there are lots of interesting theories. One of the most accepted ones is that it is the initials U and S, for United States, stuck one on top of the other—people writing the symbol in a hurry just stopped using the bottom part of the U. Another idea is that it is a mangled form of the number 8, because the Spanish coins known as "pieces of eight" were the most common coins in North America 200 years ago.

Thaler is a shortened form of *Joachimsthaler*, the name of a coin that came from a silver mine in the German town of Joachimsthal.

Chinese coins had a hole in the middle, so they could be tied onto a string.

Stringing Along

We get the word "cash" from the ancient Chinese, who carried their coins in bundles on string. A bundle of a hundred coins was called one *cash*. But the Chinese didn't invent the word, either—they got it from the Portuguese, with whom they traded, and who called their coins *caixa* (pronounced "cash-a").

Money Around the World
FROM A TO Z

austral	Argentina
birr	Ethiopia
cordoba	Nicaragua
dong	Vietnam
euro	European Community
forint	Hungary
guilder	Aruba
hryvana	Ukraine
inti	Peru
Jamaican dollar	Jamaica
kuna	Croatia
lekë	Albania
metical	Mozambique
ngultrum	Bhutan
ouguiya	Mauritania
pataca	Macao
quetzal	Guatemala
ruble	Russia
shilling	Kenya
tugrik	Mongolia
U.S. dollar	United States
vatu	Vanuatu
won	Republic of Korea
x	Marks the spot
yen	Japan
zloty	Poland

CHECK it out!

There may not be a currency that begins with X, but that doesn't mean that X amount of money is worthless! An X, to show precise coordinates, is the way buried treasure is marked on a map. The word "sawbuck" means a ten-dollar bill because of X: a sawbuck is a makeshift table consisting of a flat board sitting on two X-shaped legs, and the letter X is the Roman numeral for ten.

Shekel was the name of a silver coin used in Biblical times (see below). Though the word is used in North American slang to mean dollar, it is the name of real money once again. In 1980, the people of Israel started officially calling their money shekels (see above).

Speaking Slang-uages

In every language there are slang terms for money—or the lack of it. If you had a dollar for every nickname money has, you'd be rich. Dollars are sometimes called "bucks," for the days when North American Native peoples used buckskins, or deerhides, for trade. A hundred years ago, you'd have heard North American money being called "saddle blankets" because the bank notes were very large—large enough, people joked, to cover a horse's back. In Latin America, money is nicknamed "little paper." In France, money is "the ticket" or "the round stuff." In Germany it's known as "pinke-pinke," for the sound coins make as they jingle in your pocket.

18

Hot As a Pistol

Explorers, settlers, and immigrants helped shape some of the many nicknames for money used in North America. You may have heard money called "moolah"—and if you wonder why, you're not alone. Popular in the 1920s and 1930s in the United States, "moolah" was one of the many terms in the rich language of jazz musicians. Perhaps it came from Africa, as did so many of the other jazz words used by African-Americans. But nobody really knows.

Because the Spanish ruled both North and South America for so long, it's not surprising that Spanish-sounding words are still used in modern English. *Pistoles* is one; it comes from the name of an old Spanish coin made of gold.

From the Yiddish-speaking Jews of Europe we get "mazuma." It comes from the Hebrew word *mezumman*, which means "fixed," probably meaning that each note or coin was of a fixed amount. The Yiddish word for five is *finf*, and over the years it came to be pronounced "fin," a slang name for the five-dollar bill.

An American quarter is sometimes called "two bits." This expression goes back to old Spanish coins called pieces of eight (see below). These coins could be cut into as many as eight pieces. Because two pieces would be worth one quarter of the whole coin, "two bits" came to mean a quarter of a dollar, too.

money myth

The ancient Romans believed that after people die, their souls go to live in the underworld. The long voyage involves crossing the River Styx, which divides the world of the living from the world of the dead, by taking a ferry run by Charon, the guardian of the underworld. And he doesn't do it for free. When a Roman died, the family would put a gold coin into her mouth so she would have something to give the ferryman. The Chinese thought the afterworld was like this one, so a spirit would need money there. They still print up special bank notes to be burned when a body is cremated.

CHECK it out!

If you work for a living, you are paid a salary, which literally means you are given salt. It comes from the days when salt was hard to get and much prized. Roman soldiers were given an allowance to buy salt from the merchants who traded in it. This allowance was called a *salarium*.

Money Hungry

Food terms often stand in for money because—let's face it—if you don't have any money, chances are you don't eat.

bacon	as in "bring home the bacon;" to earn money
beans	nothing; what Jack got instead of money in *Jack and the Beanstalk*
berries	sweet stuff
bickies	Australian nickname for biscuits, or cookies; sweet stuff
blé	French for wheat, like "bread" and "dough"
bread	have money to buy bread; also English Cockney rhyming slang: bread and honey = money
dough	same idea as bread
greens	from the color of some bills
grub stake	an investment; a miner in Australia and North America would get his grub, or food, free from store-owners who expected to be repaid when the miner found gold
lettuce	same as greens
lolly	from lollipop; sweet stuff
pasta	used in Spain
plum	an old English word for £100,000
radis	French word for "radish;" used when there's no money, as in "I'm so broke I don't even have a radish."
sausage	English Cockney rhyming slang: sausage and mash = cash (mash are mashed potatoes)

Famous Faces

The English were the main settlers of North America from the 17th century on. In England, a six-penny coin was known as a "simon." When the English were battling the French for control of North America, they would make fun of the French emperor, Napoleon. Some wise guy put "simon" and "Napoleon" together and came up with the word "simoleon," which today still means a dollar.

In urban American slang, bank notes are sometimes called "dead presidents" for the historic figures whose portraits are on different bills. A General or a Grant—after General Ulysses S. Grant—is $50. A Benjamin stands for Benjamin Franklin and is worth $100. George Washington is worth a single buck, while an Abe (for Abraham Lincoln) might be five dollars, or just a plain old copper penny.

For many Americans, a George Washington sighting on a $1 bill might be an everyday occurrence, but seeing Benjamin Franklin is a little more rare.

Market day at Covent Garden, London, was a bustling scene of early British commerce.

The Craziest Money in the World

For centuries, Britain had the most complicated currency anyone has ever seen. There were three different units of measurement: the pound, the shilling, and the pence. A pound was made up of 20 shillings, and a shilling was made up of 12 pence.

To add to the fun, the symbols used were £ (pound), s (shilling), and d (pence)! The d stood for *denarius*, Latin for the most common silver coin in the Roman Empire.

The currency lent itself to a colorful language of names and nicknames. The farthing, from the old English word for fourth (*farden*) was a quarter of a penny, a ha'penny was a half penny, while tuppence meant two pennies. A shilling was known as a bob, and a florin, or two shillings, was a two-bob bit. It certainly simplified things when, in 1971, the English system went decimal, and the country cut back to a simple 100 pennies to the pound. But it did mean an end to some fun with language.

WHAT'S THE WHAT?

The British call their pound a "quid," Latin for the word "what." It might mean that if you have a quid, you have *what* it takes to pay for *what*ever you need. A guinea—made of gold from the African country of Guinea—was meant to be worth one pound when it was first made, but it wound up being worth more because of the value of the gold it was made from. Traditionally, one pound meant one pound of silver, and both a guinea and a quid were supposed to be worth one pound. But sometimes they were and sometimes they weren't, depending on what the price of silver was compared to gold. So a guinea became one pound plus one shilling. Ordinary people did business in pounds, but gentlemen and aristocrats always dealt in guineas. No wonder if you asked an Englishman for £1 he'd say, "What?"

CHAPTER 3

MAKING

MONEY

Minting Coins and Printing Notes

ave you ever heard the expression "Money doesn't grow on trees?" It's true there aren't any parks graced by shady trees with leaves of crisp dollar bills. But money does grow on trees, and on bushes, and even under the ground, too.

Trees give us wood pulp, which is used to make paper. The bushes are cotton and flax, whose leaves give us cotton and linen cloth, which also goes into paper. And paper is what money is printed on.

And what about the underground "treasure"—the metal ores that are minted into coins? Coins have been around much longer than paper money. They're harder and tougher and last almost forever. Museums and private collectors still have coins that were made thousands of years ago.

Read on to find out all about the actual making of money.

Old coins were made by hand, usually using a hammer and a pair of dies to press a design into the coin's surfaces. This die was used to produce commercial copper tokens circulated in and around Montreal in the 1830s and 1840s.

Cold, Hard Cash

The first coins were made thousands of years ago by the Lydians, out of a mixture of gold and silver called electrum. The Lydians didn't have complicated machinery to do their work for them, so they made their coins by hand. First they made a "die," a hard stamp with a design carved into it backward. They softened the electrum by heating it; then, while the metal was like putty, they would press down on it very hard with the die and let it leave its mark.

The Lydians' coins were unevenly shaped—different in thickness and size. The ancient Greeks made their coins even by pouring the hot metal into round molds then striking each coin with the die, using a hammer to pound the image in deep. The Romans hammered silver or gold strips into the proper shape and thickness. They then put two dies together on a hinge, squeezing hard against both sides of the metal to make coins that were marked front and back.

MAKING A MINT

A great advance in coin-making happened in the middle of the 17th century. Mints became more mechanized as new kinds of machinery were invented. Instead of being hammered, coins were made by mills—giant rolling pins squeezing bars of metal down until they were thin enough to work with.

A hundred years later there was another breakthrough, when a type of steel that was hard enough for pressing was invented. With this amazing new metal, copies of the master die could be made so that many more coins could be printed at once. Until then, minting coins had been a time-consuming, painstaking process.

The *Chameau* was one French ship that didn't make it. It went down in 1725. Its wrecked remains were found in the 1960s, including cases of gold coins still in good condition after more than 200 years at the bottom of the sea.

Help! Send Money!

There were often shortages of coins, especially in the colonies of the New World. Some of the North American settlers took matters into their own hands. In Massachusetts, a small, secret mint was built that produced coins from 1652 to 1682. For the entire 30 years, all the coins made at this mint were dated 1652 so that the government in London wouldn't catch on to what the colonists were up to.

The people of New France, part of the vast territories during the 17th and 18th centuries that would eventually become Canada, were constantly in need of coins. Early settlers exchanged furs they had trapped to buy what they needed. But as teachers, priests, and farmers arrived, barter was no longer enough. They needed money. The king of France sent ships full of coins across the Atlantic, but not often enough to meet the demand. And sometimes the ships, like the *Chameau* (right), didn't arrive at all. Quite a few sank in the dangerous waters of the North Atlantic.

Things didn't get better after the British took control of the area. Even though the English had been making coins since before Roman times, they didn't think much of the colonies' need for coins. They could spare only old copper pennies, so worn down and battered they were practically useless.

RECOVERED TREASURE
FROM
Le Chameau
PUBLIC AUCTION · FRIDAY AND SATURDAY · DECEMBER 10 AND 11 · 1971

LOST 26 AUGUST 1725
Port Nova Island, Kelpy Cove,
Nova Scotia, Canada

Ye Olde Mint

After the Americans won their independence from Britain, they set up their own mint in Philadelphia in 1792 to make coins for their new country: the United States. The newly independent Americans were in such a rush to strike their own coins that they couldn't wait for their mint. The first United States coin was actually struck in the cellar of a man named John Harper the day before the mint began operations. It was called a half-dime. Canadians, still loyal to England, didn't get their own mint until 1900.

How the Jingle Gets to Jangle

Coins were once valuable in themselves and accepted in trade because they were made of valuable metal. But all that changed in the 20th century, as precious metals became rarer and more expensive. The coins we use now are valuable because the governments that issue them say they are, and we believe it.

Coins today are made of a variety of mixed metals. The coin called a nickel in the United States isn't made of pure nickel—it may also contain copper, zinc, brass, bronze, or aluminum. But when you put the correct change in a vending machine to buy a can of soda pop, the machine will give it to you. How does it know you put in the right coins? It "reads" every coin's value from its weight and size, the thickness of its edge, and the electrical properties of the metals in it.

money myth

According to French tradition, the way to find money is to put a lizard's tail in your shoes before setting out on an adventure. English superstition says that you will always have money if you keep a bent silver coin in your pocket. But you have to remember to take it out every new moon and spit on it.

When the United States Mint was created in 1792, anyone working there who wrecked the coins, made fake ones, or stole the real ones would be punished by death.

CHECK it out!

The Royal Australian Mint not only makes coins for the land Down Under, but also for Papua New Guinea, Tonga, Samoa, Fiji, Malaysia, Thailand, Nepal, Bangladesh, and Israel.

JUST PLAIN LOONIE

The new Canadian one-dollar coin was designed to go into circulation in 1987. It was to show a French explorer and a Native guide paddling a canoe. The two men in a canoe were supposed to make a simple trip: from the Canadian Mint's headquarters in Ottawa to the mint's factory in Winnipeg. The explorers, in the form of dies and molds about the size of toy building blocks, were packed for their journey in boxes, but the boxes never arrived at their destination. No one knows if they were stolen or just lost.

In case counterfeiters had stolen the dies and molds, the government didn't want to take chances. The decision was made to change the design altogether, at a cost of $24,000. So instead of the explorers on their one-dollar coin, Canadians wound up with a diving bird called a loon. The shiny gold "loonies" have been a great big hit. Who knows what the coins would have been called if the explorers hadn't lost their way?

The Modern Mint

Modern mints aren't very high-tech, and a lot depends on human hands and eyes. Coin-making hasn't changed all that much in 200 years. The metals are weighed, melted down, and poured into molds. Then they are rolled out to the right thickness, and blanks are punched out with what looks like a fancy cookie-cutter. The blanks are heated, then cooled to soften the metal. Their edges are raised and the rims are marked. Then both sides of the coins are stamped, and they're ready.

It may not sound too complicated, but think about this: at the United States Mint in Philadelphia, 20 million coins are made *a day*. In Canada, it's nearly 3 million coins a day—that's 700 million pennies in one year. For euro launch day on January 1, 2002, Europe minted 8.15 billion shiny new coins. That's a lot of change!

Machines and human hands and eyes weigh the finished coins, examine them, count them out, and put them into bags for shipment to the banks.

Your Money's No Good Around Here!

The history of making money has seen some expensive mistakes. Not all money is popular once it's been printed, and a government can't force people to use money they don't like. In 1954, a new Canadian one-dollar bill was issued. People found something terribly wrong with the portrait of Queen Elizabeth II on the right-hand side of the note. The curls and waves in her hair right above her ear seemed to make up a face. Some said it was the face of the devil. The government tried to assure Canadians that the plate-making artist did not intend to make the queen's hair into the devil. But people rejected the note, superstitious about using "spooky" money. So the bills were taken out of circulation.

CHECK it out!

Americans say something is phony "as a two-dollar bill." Canadians say it's phony "as a three-dollar bill."

Canadians said "no" to this one-dollar bill issued in 1954.

The new U.S. one-dollar coin, called by some a "Sac" or a "Sacky," looks like it might be here to stay.

In 1976, the American government printed a new two-dollar bill. There had been two-dollar bills before, but they had gone out of use. When the new bills came out, no one would touch them. Banks gave people change in twos, and people would demand ones or fives instead. One enterprising bank in the state of Indiana tried offering the two-dollar bill for only $1.95. Even that didn't work. No one can really explain why Americans didn't like the two-dollar bill, but it was clear that they didn't want anything to do with it. The government tried again in 1999, and this time there wasn't as much of a fuss. Americans might still look at the two-dollar bill as an oddity, but there are 583 million of them out there.

A similar thing happened to a one-dollar coin the U. S. minted in 1979. It was called the Susan B. Anthony dollar, in honor of one of the country's most famous feminists. "No, thanks," Americans said once again, and the last one was struck by the U. S. Mint in 1981. The U. S. Mint tried again in 1999, with a gold-colored one-dollar coin carrying a portrait of the Native explorer Sacagawea. This one looks like it might stay around. But the United States government hasn't withdrawn one-dollar bills, the way the Canadian and Australian governments did when they introduced the one-dollar coin, so Americans can still choose paper over metal.

Movie Money

When a coin or bill goes out of circulation, it's usually useful only to collectors and museums for its historical value. But the people who lived on Fanning Island during World War II found an unusual use for their old money.

Fanning Island is in the South Pacific near Australia. When the war broke out, there were 740 people living on the island, all of them employed picking and shipping out coconuts for Fanning Island Plantations Limited. They used Australian money, but with the Japanese threatening the Pacific, they were cut off from Australia. As the supply of cash dwindled on the island, the workers couldn't be paid, and people couldn't do business.

One of the plantation managers asked the American army in the area to have bank notes printed in Hawaii. The notes were signed by the plantation manager and were valid only on Fanning Island.

At the end of the war, Fanning Island went back to using Australian notes. The plantation money was recalled and each bill was cut down the middle to show it was no longer any good. But it seemed a shame to waste it. So the people of Fanning Island found something else to do with it. They all went to the movies, using the cut-up plantation notes as admission tickets.

The Real Thing

All paper money is very carefully made in high security plants. It has to be. If you were handed a five-dollar bill that didn't look or feel right, you'd know right away that you couldn't take it to the store or put it into the bank. You wouldn't trust that money, and you wouldn't trust the person who gave it to you. And you'd know that if you tried to give that five dollars to someone else, he wouldn't trust you. So bank note printers have to make sure that whatever they produce will be accepted as good money.

They also have to make the money difficult to copy. If everyone could pull out a blank sheet of paper and draw "money" on it with inks and paints, real money wouldn't be worth very much, because no one could ever be sure it was real. That's why every bank note looks very complicated, with curlicues in the corners, different colors laid over each other, finely detailed drawings of people or birds or animals, and lots of numbers in odd places.

The Color of Money

It is decidedly easier to fly to the moon and back than it is to find out how any one printing plant mixes its inks. You might think all United States bills are green—but think again. The parts that are green are a mix of a bit of blue, a bit of gray, and a bit of black. In 2003, the United States Bureau of Engraving and Printing added a touch of peach to the new $20 bill, shocking the nation.

If you tilt a greenback or any other bank note in the light, the green will look black, the black will look green, or each color might have a hint of red or gold. That's because the ink has tiny flakes of metal added to it so that light plays off the combination of colors, just like sunlight does on a butterfly's wing. This lovely effect is called "color shifting."

The more details you put on a bank note, the more difficult it is for any person trying to copy it to get all the details right.

Particular Paper

The paper that bank notes are printed on has to be of a certain quality, thickness, and finish. Each country keeps the formula it uses to make its paper a closely guarded secret. But if you look at and feel several different currencies, you'll notice a difference. Some papers are coarse and feel like a worn-out towel, others are silky like the softest bedsheet.

The United States Bureau of Engraving and Printing uses a printing process that actually presses the design into the paper with great force. You can also see tiny red and blue flecks that look like loose threads scattered about the face of a U. S. bill; these are part of the secret formula of the papermaking.

Many different countries use a watermark on their bills—a shadowy face or design in the paper itself, which you can see only if you hold the bank note up against the light. English pounds, and Canadian and American dollars, are among the many bank notes that contain something you can't see with your naked eye: a metallic thread running through the paper. This security thread is made of very thin aluminum foil wrapped in cellophane. Although you can't see it in normal light, special black light or ultraviolet light-bulbs, make the thread glow red through the paper.

CHANGE IS GOOD

Bank note printers change color and design to keep counterfeiters on their toes. They've added holograms, color tones that photocopiers can't copy, fine lines that turn into a messy blur if you try to run them through a scanner, images that can be seen only at certain angles, magnetic inks, tiny rectangles of silver or gold foil, touchable bumps for the visually impaired to identify the note—they have even considered adding a microchip that will emit a radio frequency. The bad news: counterfeiters managed to pass off U. S. $47.5 million in fake money in 2001, despite all the new protections in bank notes. The good news: that's only 0.02 per cent, or 2 in every 10,000 genuine bills.

Certain details visible only under ultraviolet light help distinguish genuine from counterfeit bank notes.

Put It on Paper

The Bank of Canada issues about 800 million notes, or bills, a year. The presses at the United States Bureau of Engraving and Printing use 32 tons of special paper made of cotton and linen fibers and 6 tons of ink every 24 hours. The one-dollar notes are printed on sheets. There are 32 notes per sheet, and 8,000 sheets are made in one hour.

The Bank of England Printing Works makes its own inks—200 tons a year. The workers there get to listen to rock music on loud-speakers as thousands of pound notes in denominations of £5, £10, £20, and £50 roll off the presses. In one recent year, 955,000,000 bills were made.

At the U. S. Bureau of Engraving and Printing, 37 million notes roll off the presses in one day. Almost half are one-dollar bills.

Proper Printing

There are three different ways to print paper money. The first is to press the paper hard against a stone or a sheet of firm rubber that has been marked with a pattern. The second is to cut away from the rubber everything but the design you want to print, then dip it in ink and press it against the paper—like a rubber stamp or a toy printing set.

The third way involves cutting the pattern deep into soft steel plates, which are then inked very heavily. The printing leaves a thick layer of ink on the paper. Most bank notes around the world are made using this last process, called *intaglio*, because it is the hardest for anyone but a professional printer to do.

CHECK it out!

Computers have added another dimension to printing money: teeny, tiny letters invisible to the naked eye, called "micro-printing." On the 1996 version of the United States $100 bill, the number 100 is stamped on the top and bottom. These numbers look like they are filled with curvy lines—and they are, except for the one on the lower left. If you put that 100 under a powerful microscope, you could read "USA 100" up and down inside the number, over and over and over again.

For the Birds

Did you know that the bird pictured on American money was a real eagle named Peter? In the early days of the United States Mint, the people who worked there adopted him to use as a model for the drawings and as a pet.

You can always tell what kind of mood the Americans are in by what the eagle is doing on the currency. These days, he sits on a shield with his wings folded, holding the olive branch of peace in one talon and the arrows of war in the other. But in the past, he has been shown swooping angrily through the sky (when America felt threatened) or sitting peacefully and majestically (when America felt on top of the world).

A REALLY BIG BILL

The largest denomination ever printed at the United States Bureau of Engraving and Printing was a $100,000 bill with a portrait of President Woodrow Wilson— 42,000 were issued just once. But ordinary people never saw one. The notes were made specially for the Federal Reserve System so that it could transfer large amounts of money from one branch of the central bank to another, or from one branch of government to another. The Federal Reserve decided one day it was much simpler to keep written records of the transfers rather than pass an actual $100,000 bill around.

The last of the big bills. Computers have made it much easier to simply transfer large amounts of money electronically.

New Money, Old Money

Not only do engravers work with incredible precision, but they do it backward! The design they cut into the plates is the mirror image of what it will look like when it is printed.

Each and every bank note is a tiny work of art. A lot of thinking goes into the decision of what to put on a bill. Most of the elements you see have always been a part of bank note design: pictures of important people or buildings, flowers or animals, official seals and signatures.

Bank notes come in all sorts of beautiful colors, and all are beautifully drawn. Even though many of the elements of the designs are done on computers, the drawings you see on the bills are still cut into the plates used to print them by master craftspeople called engravers. Working from the designs of an artist, the engravers capture every feather on a bird, every hair on a person's head, and every dot and dash and squiggly line around a number, all with incredible precision. No wonder it takes 12 to 15 years of training to become an engraver.

Euro-Money, My Money

If you had a chance to design a bank note from scratch, what would *you* put on it? Your dog? Your house? Your dad? That's the question the European countries had to answer when they agreed to stop using a different kind of money for each country in the European Union and come up with something that everyone would like. It took them ten years, and people are still arguing about whether they got it right.

WHERE OLD MONEY GOES TO DIE

The average five-pound note lasts about a year before it becomes worn and threadbare. The dollar fares a bit better—it has a life of 15 to 18 months. On the average, a one-dollar bill is passed 500 times before it wears out. A five-dollar bill is used only about 300 times and lasts a bit longer—about two years. The $20 bill is passed 400 times and stays in circulation for five years.

Almost everywhere in the world, if you find yourself with a bank note that's thin or torn or messed up in any way, you can take it to a local bank and exchange it for a crisp, new one.

But where does old money go when it dies? Most of it goes up in smoke. The banks ship the old bills back to the printing plant. There they are inspected by sophisticated electronic equipment as well as human eyes to make sure that they aren't reusable, and that they're not fakes that were good enough to make it past the bank's eyes. Then they're bundled up, shredded, and thrown into the fire. Some countries, notably England, stopped doing that when they decided using shredded pound notes as landfill was better for the environment.

The fifteen members of the European Union at the time had eleven languages and two different alphabets between them. And rather than get into fights about whether to have my king or your prime minister on the money, the designers chose to go without people at all. They chose neutral subjects like famous bridges on one side and historical styles of architecture on the other. The word "euro" appears both in Latin (EURO) and Greek letters (EYPO), and the stars in a circle that make up the flag of the European Union float over the pictures.

CHECK it out!

When euros first went out into the world on January 1, 2002, there were 14.5 billion individual notes printed to go around. The ten-, twenty-, and fifty-euro notes were the most common—about 3 billion each of those—followed by fives and 100s, at 2.5 and 1.2 billion each.

Up in Flames

Even after the Americans threw out Iraq's dictator Saddam Hussein in 2003, doing business in Iraq meant being constantly reminded of Hussein: his portrait was on every bank note. So they decided to redesign the Iraqi dinar. The new bills were printed in five different countries, including Germany, Sri Lanka, and the United Kingdom, because Iraq's own mints weren't big enough for the job. Twenty-five jumbo jets delivered the new money to Baghdad. Iraqis brought their old bills to the bank to trade in, and walked out with crisp, new Saddam-less dinars.

CHAPTER 4

MONEY IN THE BANK

Keeping It Safe

When you have money, you want to make sure that it's safe. For thousands of years, people have saved money by putting it away. Archaeologists digging up the cities of ancient Greece have found jars with holes or slits in them that were used to hold coins.

The best place to keep money today is in a bank. What is a bank? Most important, it is a place where your money is safe. If you stuff all your pennies into a purple sock in the bottom drawer of your dresser, and you're sure no one will find it, then you could call it the Purple Sock Bank and you'd be quite right. But a modern bank does more than hold your money. It's also a place where you can borrow, or make your money produce more money.

From clay pots to gleaming skyscrapers of glass and steel, banks are simply places where you put your money to keep it secure. Modern banks have become mind-bogglingly complicated, with the ability to grow money through interest rates and investments. But whether you hide your money in a purple sock or a bank account, the goal is still the same: to keep other people's sticky fingers off your stash. Here's the story of how banking became so important.

Banking on It

Try to imagine 710 billion yen (¥710, 000, 000, 000) all piled up in one place. That's how much money the Mizuho Financial Group Bank of Japan, the world's biggest bank, has to meet the needs of its customers.

What's all the action about? A bank is a place where you can do more than just store your money. It's also a place where you can borrow money or make your money produce more money.

When a lot of people put their money in a bank and they don't need all of it back right away, the bank is holding a large amount of money that can be used by others. Someone who needs cash asks the bank to lend it to him for a while; when the time's up he pays back the borrowed amount, called the "principal," plus a fee for its use. This fee is a percentage of the principal, known as "interest." The bank keeps some of the interest to pay for keeping track of who's got whose money, how much of it, and for how long— and it keeps some for profit. The rest goes back to the people who keep their money in the bank. So your money makes money—for you and the bank.

If you were to ask a banker at a Mizuho branch how much money goes in and out of the bank each day, she might answer, "How much air do you breathe?" It's so much that it can't be counted. Of course it is counted, but the numbers would go by so fast on a computer screen you'd think you had entered *The Matrix*.

Museums hold the clay tablets on which Babylonian priest bankers wrote who had deposited money, and how much.

International Banking

In Babylon nearly 5,000 years ago, people thought the safest place to keep their money was with the priests at the temples. But anyone who could get his or her hands on enough cash could be a banker. One of the oldest records of a loan was written out by a family named Egibi. They loaned out "2/3rds of a mann of silver" and expected one shekel per month as interest from the borrower.

The Greeks, Romans, and the ancient Chinese all had some form of banking system. Their main purpose was to keep peoples' money safe, and to lend it to those who could afford to pay it back with interest. But they also performed another important function: keeping track of how much all kinds of foreign money was worth. Traders from the city of Rome might sell their goods to merchants in the city of Pisa and be paid with coins that looked different from the ones they used at home. So the bank in Rome would weigh the gold from Pisa, judge its purity, and give the Roman traders Roman coins in exchange for it.

ZERO THE HERO

Roman banks and the early banks of Europe that used the Roman system of counting didn't have an easy time keeping track of their money. Roman numerals are letters—just try multiplying LVII by CXXIX! To make matters even more complicated, try doing addition, multiplication, or subtraction without using a zero. It's hard to believe, but for many centuries, the zero was unknown in Europe. Mathematicians in India had invented the zero hundreds of years before, along with the numerals from 1 to 9. They passed this knowledge on to the Arabs, who adopted it as their own system.

In the 1200s, an Italian trader named Leonardo Fibonacchi finally introduced the Arabic way of counting to his native country. It revolutionized the way banks did business. Keeping track of amounts coming in and going out became much easier—and more exact.

CHECK it out!

You might save your pennies in a bank that's shaped like a pig. The story of today's piggy banks goes back about a thousand years. In England, a kind of red clay used to make pots was called *pygg*. After several hundred years of people using *pygg* pots to keep their coins in, a clever potter decided to make the pot look like its name sounded: a pig.

Going National

In Europe all through the 15th and 16th centuries, any number of people called themselves bankers. Goldsmiths and jewelers had safe boxes, could judge the purity of a coin, and could trade the coins of one country for those of another.

The first national bank, created and run by a government, was the Bank of Amsterdam, founded in 1609. At that time, the tiny country of Holland was becoming a great trading nation, shipping spices from the Orient and gold and silver from the New World into Europe. There were 14 private mints in Holland, and there was very little control over the silver coins they made. The coins were easy to counterfeit by melting them down and mixing the silver with copper. Shopkeepers didn't trust anyone's money as being good—they went back to the ancient custom of keeping scales in their shops to weigh the coins.

On top of that, the trade the Dutch carried out with other nations brought so many different kinds of money into the country that no one could keep it all straight. A simple thing like buying a loaf of bread and getting the right change could set your head spinning. If you gave the baker one kind of coin in payment, he might give you five different kinds of coins as change.

When the Dutch government published a booklet in 1610 for moneychangers to help them sort it all out, it listed 341 different kinds of silver coins and 505 different gold coins in circulation in the country. So the Dutch government stepped in to clear up the confusion.

The Bank of Amsterdam was set up to control the kinds of coins that could be used in that city. Anyone bringing money into the bank could change it for the proper kinds of coins. Or they could leave it in the bank and get a receipt.

CHECK it out!

In Italy the Medicis became the wealthiest and most powerful family in Europe by lending money to the Pope, as well as to ordinary traders and merchants, at high rates of interest. In England, lawyers made it their business to know people who had money to lend so that, for a fee, they could introduce them to people who wanted to borrow it.

Governments Guarantee It

What was unusual about the Bank of Amsterdam was that the government guaranteed the depositors' money. If for some reason all the depositors wanted their money at the same time and the bank didn't have enough cash on hand, the city would pay the depositors.

The government's guarantee was an important step in the development of banking. When people put their money in a bank, they might imagine that their money sits in the bank's vaults, but in reality, each depositor's money is added to the pool from which the bank makes its loans. So some of the depositors' money is actually in the hands of borrowers. If one depositor wants her money, the bank always has enough in the vault to pay out. But if everyone wants his or her money at the same time, the bank might not have enough on hand. Without a guarantee, the bank couldn't pay all of its depositors.

Unexpected events can make people worry that their money isn't safe. That's what happened at the Bank of Amsterdam in 1672. The citizens heard that the king of France was planning to invade Holland. They panicked that they wouldn't be able to get their money out of the bank, so they all arrived at once, demanding to have their deposits back. When the bank showed that it could and would pay everyone, with the city's help, the customers changed their minds about taking their money out. They had proof that their money was safe, so they left it in the bank.

CASH ON DEMAND

Just before the American Civil War, there were so many banks in the U.S. issuing their own notes that no one could be sure what money was worth. If you had $1 stamped "City of Atlanta" you might not be able to get a dollar's worth of change at a bank in New York.

Nowadays, most old bank notes aren't worth much (except to collectors) once they're out of circulation. There is one notable exception. In 1861, at the beginning of the American Civil War, the North issued Demand Notes in denominations of $5, $10, and $20. If you had one, you could demand that amount in coins. They haven't been printed since 1862, but if you ever find one, you can still get your full money's worth in today's currency.

The U.S. Treasury's first paper currency, Demand Notes helped finance the American Civil War.

The Most Trusted Bank in the World

In 1694 a new bank opened its doors for business in London. Its official name was the Bank of England, but it became so famous and successful that most people simply called it "The Bank," as though there were no other banks anywhere else. The way it did business set the standards for banking everywhere. And it started because of a war.

The same king of France who had been threatening Holland was now threatening England. The king of England needed money to raise armies against France. A Scottish businessman named William Paterson made a deal with the English king: if the king would grant Paterson the right to run a bank, Paterson's bank would lend the government money to pay for an army. Paterson thought people would feel confident about depositing their money in a bank that was lending their money to the government, because they could be sure the government would pay the money back. The idea worked brilliantly. Only four days after The Bank opened, eager Britons had deposited £100,000. It was truly a king's ransom.

The Bank of England has been known since the 18th century as "The Old Lady of Threadneedle Street" (where it's located).

A Perspective View of the Bank of England.

New Banking Ideas

The Bank of England helped its customers to save and spend their money in new ways:

• A **Running Cash Note** was a piece of paper saying that whoever brought it in could get the coins it represented. If you put ten gold coins in the bank, you'd get the bank's note for ten gold coins. Say that you wanted to buy a telescope worth ten gold coins. You could go into the shop and say to the storekeeper, "I want to buy that telescope. I don't have ten gold coins with me, but I do have a note from the bank saying I have ten gold coins there." The storekeeper could give you the telescope and then take the note to the bank and claim the coins.

• An **Accomptable Note** worked a bit like today's bank book. It had your name on it and you, as the depositor, were the only person who could get at your money. If you wanted to give some of your money to someone else—say a toymaker—you could write a letter to the bank saying, "Please give Mr. Doll 75 pennies of my money, which is in account number 1234," and sign it. These letters were the first checks.

• A **Sealed Bill** was a receipt the bank would give you if you gave the bank your cash and promised to leave it there for a specific period of time without taking any out. At the end of that period, the bank would pay you a healthy pile of interest. This was the first example of what we now call a term deposit.

The Value of Trust

Nowadays we take paper money, checks, and term deposits for granted, but more than 300 years ago, when the Bank of England started issuing them, they were new ideas. Then some of the smaller English banks started to get into trouble because they gave out more paper money than they had coins on deposit. Quite a few of them went out of business and people started distrusting banks. But banks were useful for doing business, and their inventions made life easier.

There was still one bank everyone trusted: the Bank of England. It was agreed that only that bank's notes would be accepted from then on. Other banks could still take deposits, and issue checks and term deposit certificates, but they didn't have the right to print bank notes any more. In due time, the printing of the Bank of England's notes came under control of the government. The Bank became what is now known as a central bank. All the rest were called commercial banks.

Money Business

The Federal Reserve Bank of San Francisco (left) is one of 12 branches of the U.S. Federal Reserve System, which fixes interest rates and controls the amount of money in circulation.

In England, the central bank is still the Bank of England. In Canada, it's the Bank of Canada. The United States has the U.S. Federal Reserve System. Today most countries have both kinds of banks: one central bank and many commercial banks. The central bank is the government's bank. It issues paper money, sets interest rates, and keeps a close eye on the commercial banks. You can't open a savings account at the central bank, only at a commercial bank. They're the ones that do business with the public.

Commercial banks today handle billions and trillions and gazillions of dinars, dollars, rupees, rubles, shillings, and pounds. They work because people trust them. In most countries, governments take a strong interest in making sure they serve the public in a trustworthy way by providing strict regulations.

BREAKING THE BANK

From the Italian, we get the word "bank" to describe the place where money is stored and exchanged. During the early years of banking, the people who stored, exchanged, and lent money did their business in the public marketplace at a bench, a *banco* in Italian. So you'd take your money for safekeeping to the man at the bench, the banker. If he ran out of money or didn't deal fairly with his customers, the bench would be broken, or his *banco* would be *rotto*. That's the root of our word "bankrupt," which means to have no money.

Balancing the Books

To stay in business, a bank has to balance its books. Let's invent a bank; we'll call it the First Amazing Bank. If you drew a line down the middle of a piece of paper, on one side you'd write how much the bank owes other people, its *liabilities*. These include the money the bank borrowed so it could set up its business, as well as the deposits of its customers—large corporations, small companies, individuals, and even other banks.

On the other side of the line, you'd put how much money the bank has and the money others owe to it. These are its *assets*, including all the cash in the vault, certificates that can be converted to cash very easily, loans that customers will pay back, plus the value of the bank's own building, furniture, and equipment.

The total of the numbers on the assets side of the page should be at least equal to (or greater than) the total on the liabilities side of the page. If they're not, the books don't balance and the First Amazing Bank would be bankrupt. That's how it is for all banks, no matter how many billions they're dealing with. If people find out that a bank can't balance its books, they'll take their money out.

CHECK it out!

A modern coin counting machine can count 2,500 coins a minute. A bank note counting machine can tally up 100 bills in 4 seconds, and tell what denomination they are or if they are fakes.

MONEY BURNS A HOLE

When you go to the bank, the person you deal with is a teller. The word comes from an old way of counting money, called tallying. Two hundred years ago, instead of giving a written receipt, people sometimes used a piece of wood, called a tally stick (from the French word *taille*, which means a notch or a cut). When someone lent out money, he would write the borrower's name and the date on both the left and the right sides of the stick, marking each half with a notch for the amount. Then the stick was split down the middle. The borrower took one half of the stick as a bill, and the lender kept the other as a receipt. When the loan was paid back, the two halves of the stick could be compared. If they matched, they "tallied," a word we still use to mean a sum has worked out right. This system was used all over Europe, but in 1826, the English treasury started to use written records instead of tally sticks.

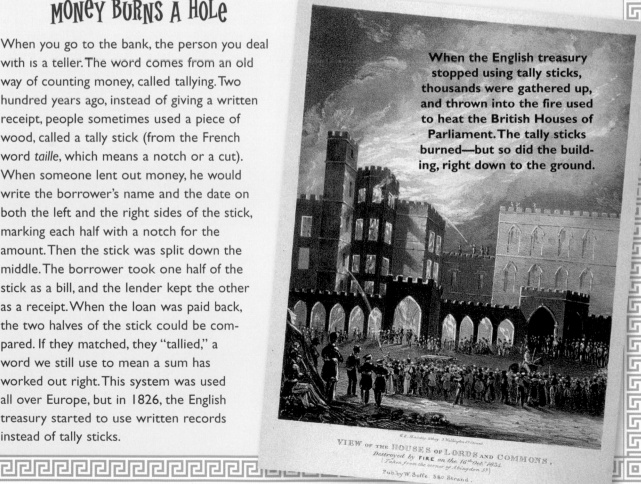

When the English treasury stopped using tally sticks, thousands were gathered up, and thrown into the fire used to heat the British Houses of Parliament. The tally sticks burned—but so did the building, right down to the ground.

VIEW OF THE HOUSES OF LORDS AND COMMONS, *Destroyed by* FIRE *on the 16th Oct. 1834.*
(Taken from the corner of Abingdon St.)
Pub. by W. Soffe, 380 Strand.

Taking It to the Bank

Wherever you bank and however much you bank, keeping your money in a safe place is a good habit to get into.

Usually banks have a big central room called the banking hall, where most business is done. There will be automatic banking machines near the front door—you can do almost all your banking at them once you've opened your account. There may be offices around the banking hall where customers can speak to staff members in private about borrowing money, or anything else they want to keep to themselves.

A sign will tell you where you should go to open a new account. If you need to wait in line to go up to a teller's window, don't forget to smile for the closed-circuit television cameras. Even if you don't see them, you can be sure they're keeping track of who comes in and goes out—just in case of unwelcome visitors.

The bank teller will ask you some questions to help you decide what sort of account you need. Many banks welcome young people as customers and have special kinds of accounts to help kids learn to manage their money. Some have a kids' banking area in the hall, websites just for younger customers, even savings clubs that give out stickers and prizes for maintaining or increasing your balance.

The bank vault is where all the money and other valuable items, stored in safe-deposit boxes, are kept. It is usually out of sight.

CHECK it out!

A vault door installed in a bank in Kansas City in 1921 weighed 45,454 kg (100,000 lbs) and needed a tractor, two five-ton trucks, and four horses to get it into place. It is still in use.

46

On Account of Saving

Most people's first bank accounts are savings accounts. When you open your first savings account, you'll get a bankbook with your name and account number on it. Inside, the bank prints how much money you have put into that account. The teller will then ask you for your signature on a piece of paper, which is filed away so that whoever you deal with at the bank will be able to check how you sign your name. That way, both you and the bank ensure that you, and only you, can take your money out.

You will also get a card for the bank's automatic tellers, and you will select your Personal Identification Number (PIN). The bank people will show you how to take money out, put it in, and update your bankbook automatically at the machine.

Savings accounts give you interest—that is, they pay you to keep your money in the account. The bank helps you keep track of your money by updating your passbook or sending you a statement so you can see what you're spending, what you're depositing, and what the bank itself is adding to your stash.

Checking into Checks

You usually have to be 18 or older to open a checking account, get a credit card, or apply for a loan. But there are a few banks run especially for kids where you can get these services as long as a responsible adult co-signs your application and guarantees that you will run your finances according to the bank's rules. A checking account works much the same way as a savings account, but instead of a bankbook, the teller will give you a checkbook. Inside are some checks with the number of your account and, at some banks, your name and address printed on them. And instead of the bank paying you interest for allowing it to keep your money, you pay the bank each month for processing your checks.

A checking account gives you easier access to your money through either a debit card or paper checks. But if you don't have enough when you make a debit payment, the bank will tell the store not to accept your card. If you write a check without the funds to cover it, the check will turn into "rubber" and "bounce" right back to you. It's not as fun as it sounds—it'll cost you both bank fees and embarrassment.

How Does Your Money Grow?

Take a seed of $100, plant it at the bank, and forget about it for a year. At very low interest rates, it will have grown to anywhere between $101 and $104. Leave it there longer and your money will just keep on making you more money, and that's because of a magic bean called *compound interest*.

Let's say you take $1,000 dollars to the Friendly Neighborhood Bank (FNB). The FNB is offering a rate of 10% interest per year—which is friendly, since interest rates are not usually that high (but it will let us keep the math easy). The FNB can pay that as either simple interest or compound interest. You choose compound interest? Good choice! And here's why.

Simple Simon

With simple interest, each year you get 10% of your *original* amount; in your case, 10% of $1,000 is $100. In ten years, you will have made ten annual interest payments of $100 each, or $1,000 in interest. Add that to your original deposit of $1,000, and you end up with $2,000. You've doubled your money in ten years. Not bad, but wait. You can do even better than that if you compound it.

CHECK it out!

The amount of money in your account at any one time is called the balance.

Compound That

With compound interest, the interest is calculated on a different amount every year—a larger amount. For the first year, you will get 10% of $1,000, or $100 interest, just like with simple interest. But then things get interesting. For the second year, you now have $1,000 plus $100 in your account, and so the interest is calculated on that $1,100. So, for your second year, you get $110 in interest, and you end up with $1,210 in your account. For the third year, your interest is 10% of $1,210, or $121; add that to your $1,210 and you get $1,331. Here's how it looks over 10 years:

	Balance	Interest	New Balance
Year 1	$1,000	$100	$1,100
Year 2	$1,100	$110	$1,210
Year 3	$1,210	$121	$1,331
Year 4	$1,331	$133	$1,464
Year 5	$1,464	$146	$1,610
Year 6	$1,610	$161	$1,771
Year 7	$1,771	$177	$1,948
Year 8	$1,948	$195	$2,143
Year 9	$2,143	$214	$2,357
Year 10	$2,357	$236	$2,593

At the end of ten years, you will have made almost $600 more with compound interest than you would have in the same amount of time with simple interest!

ADD IT TO THE COLLECTION

A good investment could be as simple as collecting something you love. Collectors can spend incredible amounts of money to get their hands on the right comic book, doll, lunch box, vinyl record album, or star's autograph. Sometimes they'll pay too much in what is known as the Bigger Fool Theory—if *you're* crazy enough to spend big bucks, out there is someone crazier who will buy the item from you for even more!

CHAPTER 5

ELECTRONIC

MONEY

Now You See It, Now You Don't

omputers have changed the way money works forever. You could, in theory, go through your whole life making money, spending it, and paying bills without ever actually touching a paper bill or a coin.

Banks had already used computers to handle their own money for many years. Then one brilliant invention after another—ATMs, magnetic coding on cards, the Internet—came barreling along at the end of the 20th century. It made more and more sense to make banking easier by connecting customers to their money digitally.

Say your grandmother wants to give you some money for your birthday. She "goes" to her bank via her computer at home and tells it to send money to your account. The next time you stop by an ATM and ask for your balance, you will see that it has gone up by the amount that Grandma put in for you. Then you can go to the store to buy yourself a new CD. You hand your bank card to the cashier, who swipes it through a machine connected to your bank by telephone. The machine receives a message that you have enough money in your account, so you push a few more buttons, and the price of the CD is deducted from your balance automatically.

And even though sometimes you feel that you can't touch it or see it or smell it or feel it, it's still money.

Ready, Set, Charge!

The term "credit card" was first used in 1887 by an American writer named Edward Bellamy. He looked far into the future—to the year 2000—and predicted that cash was going to disappear.

Not all his predictions were accurate but it is true that just about every adult in North America has a credit card of some sort. In fact, most North Americans have about six. The average household has 13, six issued by banks and seven issued by department stores or other businesses. Eighty per cent of young people between the ages of 18 and 20 have their own plastic.

Swipe the Stripe

That little black stripe on the back of your ATM or credit card is a whole novel in bits and bytes. The magnetic stripe, or magstripe, is made up of tiny magnets a fraction of a millimetre long that can be "written" on by pointing them in one direction or the other. Three different tracks of magnets, each .028 centimetres (.110 inches) wide, hold different information: what bank issued the card, and in what town and country; what accounts are attached to it; what currency you bank in; how much you're allowed to take out (your limit).

Credit cards are similar to ATM cards, but their magstripes carry even more information, including the card's expiration date.

OWe? OW!

Credit cards make life easy—too easy, even. They let you buy things on the spur of the moment, something you wouldn't do if you had to hand over cash all the time. But when you charge a purchase to a credit card, you are using the bank's money to pay the seller. And the bank is going to want it back. If you can't pay all or part of it back at the end of the month, the bank will want something extra for their trouble: interest. Credit cards carry much higher interest rates than other loans from the bank, and the interest keeps accumulating. That's why you could get a much bigger bill than you did the previous month, even if you didn't buy anything in the meantime. Before you take on a credit card, do a realistic count of how much money you have, how much you expect to get on a regular basis, how much you must spend on things every month, and how much you can play with. It's best to pay off your whole credit card bill every month.

GOING FAST

Let's say you are visiting Djakarta, Indonesia. You find a store that carries DVDs you can't find at home. "I'll take them all!" you say, grateful that you have a credit card with you. You hand over your card, and it starts an amazing, invisible journey.

By the time the store asks you to sign the credit card receipt, your information has traveled an incredible 15,794 km (9,814 miles)...in 4 seconds flat.

CHECK it out!

The most credit cards in one wallet belonged to Walter Cavanagh of Santa Clara, California. He kept 1,173 different credit cards—all of them valid—in a specially made wallet that weighed 16 kg (35 lbs) and measured 76 m (250 ft.) long.

SINGAPORE
DJAKARTA
TOWNSVILLE
SYDNEY
MELBOURNE
1 The store's card reader sends out a 150-byte message, including all the information on the magstripe, to its bank.
2 The bank adds a processing fee to the price (which the store pays) and sends the information on to the card company's data processing center in Singapore. Distance: 900 km (559 miles).
3 The data center sends a message to Melbourne, Australia, asking what bank the card is from Distance: 6,080 km (3,776 miles).
4 The main branch of your bank is in Sydney, Australia. Distance: 700 km (440 miles).
5 Sydney asks your hometown bank in Townsville, Queensland, if the cost of the DVDs is still within your spending limit. Distance: 1,690 km (1,047 miles).
6 Townsville says, "Yes." Message goes back to Singapore. Distance: 5,524 km (3,246 miles).
7 Singapore tells the store's bank in Djakarta that the transaction is approved. Distance: 900 km (559 miles).

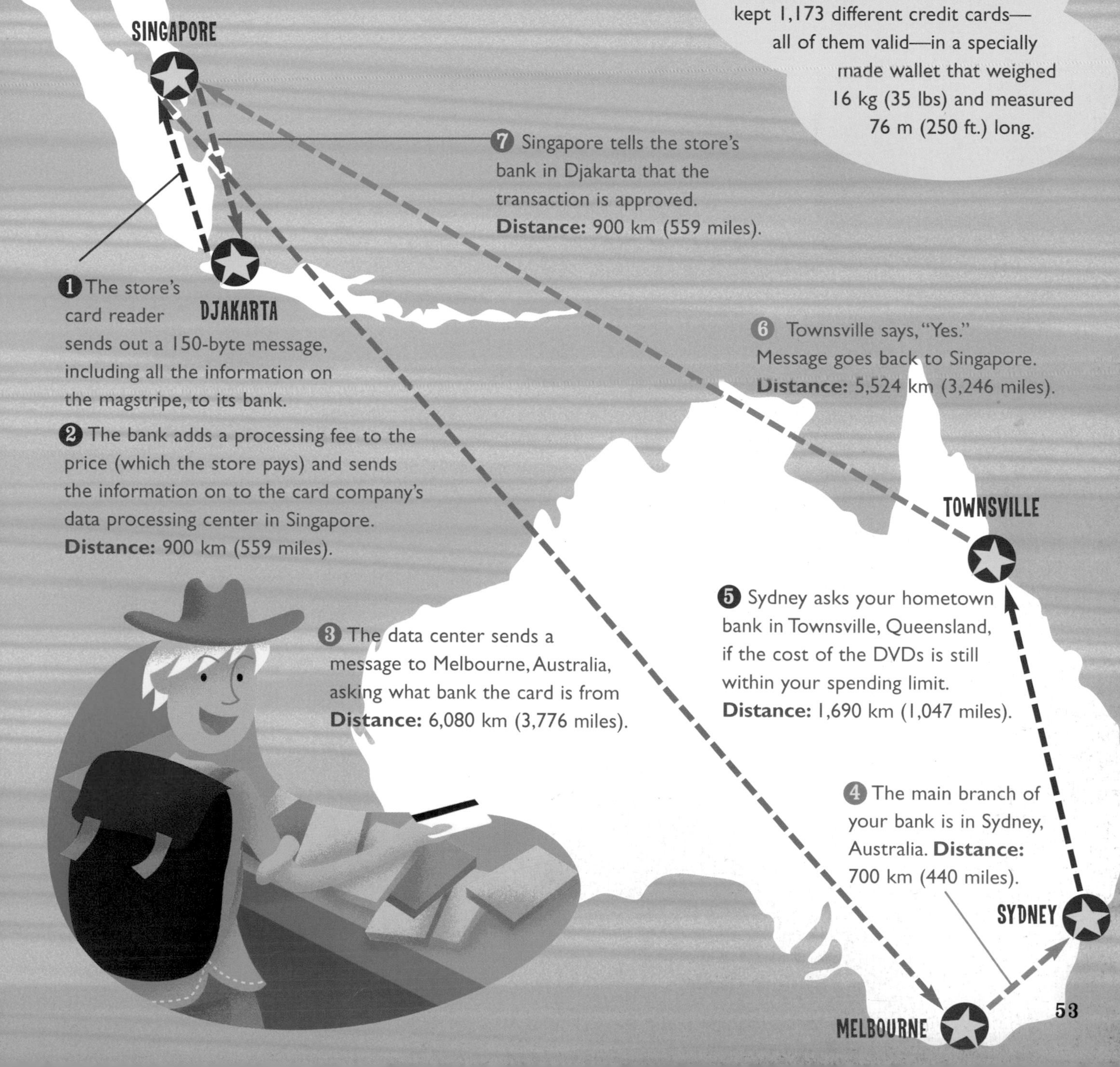

ATM—The Magic Cash Machine

When you open your bank account, the bank gives you a card that lets you use the ATM (automated teller machine).

When you go to the ATM, you put your card in, punch in your secret personal identification number (PIN), punch in how much money you want, press the button for which account the machine should access, and—presto! change-o!—your money materializes from a slot.

Have you ever thought about how an ATM actually works? In the moments it takes you to get your cash, a lot of digital magic takes place.

• The ATM is connected by a modem to a host computer that instantly reads the magnetic stripe (magstripe) on your card, making sure that your PIN and the information on the card match.

• The host computer is connected to your bank, which electronically gives the okay for the amount you want and the account you want to use.

• If you're depositing, the machine takes the deposit envelope. (Your deposit is counted later by a human being, when the machine is emptied during regular banking hours.)

• If you're withdrawing, the host computer sends an "electronic funds transfer" message to your bank to take the money out of your account and put it into the host's account.

• The host approves your transaction and your bucks are on their way out.

• Before any bills get into your hands, the machine has to count them out and keep track of them. There is an electric eye inside the machine to do the job right, as the cash goes by it on a tiny conveyor belt on its way to you.

• The details of the transaction are recorded in an electronic journal embedded in the ATM's processor. This journal can be printed out in case there is any dispute over how much money you took out.

And all this happens in about 12 seconds.

PIN HOLES

You have a Personal Identification Number (PIN) to punch in when you use an ATM. It's your signature in numbers. If you ever lose your card, a person who finds it can't simply put it in a bank machine to get your money out. The bank machine will ask for your PIN as soon as the card goes in, and if the person doesn't know it, game over.

ATM DO'S AND DON'TS

DO

• Keep your ATM card in a wallet where it won't get bent.

• Memorize your PIN number.

• Make your PIN easy for you to remember, but not obvious to others.

• Use an ATM in a well-lit public place.

• Have your ATM card in your hand before you get to the machine—searching for it at the terminal makes you more of a target for thieves.

• Get close enough to the keypad so that your body blocks anyone from seeing the numbers you type.

• Cancel your transaction and leave the machine if anyone is hovering in the area and making you uncomfortable.

• Put your cash away before you leave.

• Pick up your receipt and take it with you. You don't want other people knowing how much money you have, and you might need it if there's an error on your statement.

DON'T

• Write your PIN down and keep it anywhere near your card, especially in your wallet.

• Use your birthday, your phone number, your name, or your pet's name as your PIN—that's too easy for people who know you to figure out.

• Ever tell anyone— even your best friend—your PIN.

• Let anyone, even a friend, watch you do your ATM transaction.

• Stand too close when someone else is using the machine.

• Flash your money around.

• Litter with receipts.

• Forget to smile for the camera! Most bank premises have a security monitor that records your transaction for safety reasons.

CHECK it out!

There are almost a million ATMs in the world: about one-third in Asia and the Pacific region; less than a third in North America; a quarter in Western Europe; and the rest in Latin America, Eastern Europe, Africa, and the Middle East.

Friday is the most popular day at the ATM. The average withdrawal from an ATM is $80.

Debit Beats Credit

It's always safest to spend money you *know* you have. You can do this with cash or a debit card. A debit card may look like a credit card, but it works quite differently. When you hand over your debit card in a store, the salesperson swipes it just like a credit card. But this time, the bits and bytes tell the machine whether you have enough money in your bank account to pay for the item right away. The magstripe talks directly to your bank account, and then gives the store its permission. The salesperson hands you a keypad where the amount you're paying is displayed on top. You press the "OK" button, and type in your PIN. After a bit of a buzz and a whirr, the pair of jeans or book you want is now yours.

Debit cards are sweeping the world. And they're making checks look old-fashioned and a big bother.

CHECK it out!

Iceland leads the world in the use of plastic money, in the form of both credit cards and debit cards. Seventy per cent of all consumer business in Iceland is done with plastic, compared to 39 per cent in North America. Most Icelanders haven't seen a check for as long as they can remember. They buy movie tickets on their cellphones and pay their rent with credit cards.

BACK TO BARTER

Have you noticed how much non-money we use these days? There are airline frequent flyer points, affinity cards at bookstores and coffee shops (buy five, get one free), and reward points for phone plans, credit cards, and gas stations. And you don't always have to use your points for the obvious thing. Airline points, for example, can be used to buy flowers, rent a moving van, or stay at a hotel. Credit card points can be used to get cash back, get a gift from a catalog or, yes, buy airline tickets. And although points on any reward program don't have any cash value, the fact is you can exchange them for each other on the Web. It's like we're back to trading a cow for a blanket!

Smart Money

Cards with magstripes are good at sending information zipping down phone cables. But they're still not as smart as a smart card. You've seen them as phone cards or store gift cards. Your friend gives you a $10 gift card from a video store as a birthday present, and that means you can rent $10 worth of movies just by handing over the card. If it's reloadable, you can add value to it with cash, debit, or credit card. If not, you just throw it away.

The smart card is so smart because instead of a simple magstripe, it actually contains a microchip just like the ones in your computer. The chip can carry all sorts of details. Smart cards are great for small purchases, like an ice cream cone or a magazine. More and more, they are being used for bus and subway tickets, entrance fees at amusement parks, phone calls, and movie tickets. The latest version of the smart card has more than a microchip: it actually emits a radio frequency. Instead of signing or putting in a PIN, you tap the card against a special terminal and the terminal goes *ping* if it likes your tune. If any kind of plastic is likely to make us forget all about coins and bills, smart cards are the best bet.

HOW MUCH IS IN YOUR E-WALLET?

Buying on the Internet is big, but some people feel that giving out their credit card number online is unsafe. And no electronic merchant wants to ship you her goods just because you promise that your check's in the mail. So it was inevitable that the folks who develop clever Internet features would figure out new ways to deal with buying and selling.

Digital cash is definitely here. An e-wallet, or electronic transfer account, is an account on the Internet that is attached either to your bank account or to your credit card. When you want to send money to a merchant who also has a registered account, you simply send an e-mail to the e-wallet company with the merchant's e-mail address and the amount you wish to send. The amount will automatically be taken out of your account, and put into the account of the other person. Your credit card number is kept out of the sale.

CHAPTER 6

COPS AND ROBBERS

Other People's Money

As long as one person has money, it seems other people want to get their hands on it. Three crimes have been around as long as money itself: stealing it, faking it, and conning it out of you.

Early societies dealt with lawbreakers harshly. Thieves in the ancient world, whether they stole money or just a loaf of bread, had their hands cut off. The ancient Chinese cut out the hearts of anyone caught faking the emperor's paper currency. England holds the record for executing counterfeiters; in 1817, the British hanged 313 people for making or passing phony bank notes.

Today the penalties for robbery and counterfeiting are still pretty severe. In Canada, just trying to rob a bank—whether you get the money or not—could mean a lifetime in prison. In the United States, it carries a fine of $10,000 and 20 years in jail.

Faked money is taken seriously by governments all over the world. In Canada, making your own money could get you as much as 14 years behind bars. In the United States, you could do 15 years and pay a $5,000 fine—in government-issued bills (not the ones you made yourself). But making it isn't as serious as planning to spend money you know isn't real. If you're caught with fake bills—even if it was someone else who did the printing—the fine goes up to $15,000 and you're facing 15 years in the slammer.

Buried Treasure

Ever since people have had wealth, they've looked for ways to keep it for themselves. One way was to bury it. There are countless stories of buried treasure that is yet to be found.

In 1520, when the Aztec emperor Montezuma heard that the Spanish were heading his way, he packed a caravan of his people's treasures. He sent the gold, silver, and jewels north to be buried in the ground until the *conquistadores* (the conquerors) left. Montezuma was killed by the Spaniard Cortez, who ordered his men to take all that was left in the emperor's city. Montezuma's treasure has never been found, and some people believe it's still buried in Mexico, Arizona, or Utah.

Emperor Maximilian of Mexico was said to have buried millions in gold, silver, and precious stones near Castle Gap, Texas, before he was dethroned by angry Mexicans in the 19th century. During the American Civil War, Confederate soldiers robbed a bank in St. Albans, Vermont, burying their take somewhere near the Canadian border. Gold miners and prospectors are said to have hidden millions worth of gold in South Dakota and Colorado. For years, people with metal detectors, maps, sticks of dynamite, and shovels have tried to unearth these famous fortunes without success.

JESSE W. JAMES.
I hereby certify that the above is the only late Photograph of my deceased husband, taken before death.
MRS. JESSE W. JAMES.

Over the years, bank robbers, including Jesse James and his gang, have reportedly stashed their loot in Idaho, Indiana, and Oklahoma.

money myth

The Spanish who came to the Americas in search of wealth heard an amazing fable of a mountain tribe, who performed a ritual to honor a goddess who lived in a lake. Their king rolled in gold dust, and paddled out into the lake. He threw gold objects and emeralds into the water and then dove in to wash the gold dust off his body. The Spanish called the king El Dorado, "the golden man." They ravaged the continent in search of him and his treasure. They killed and enslaved the Native people, and stole gold from their mines and their temples, but they never found El Dorado.

More Buried Treasure

John Barkstead was an officer of the Tower of London, once one of the world's cruelest prisons. In the 1650s, he was rumored to have taken £50,000 from prisoners kept there, and buried it somewhere in the tower before he himself was executed for treason. People have searched for the treasure without any luck. If the treasure exists, it may never be found as no one is allowed to poke around anymore for fear of damaging the historic buildings.

The tower is said to hold many secrets; one is a cache of gold and jewels known as the Barkstead Treasure.

"X" Marks the Spot

In 1795, three young men paddling a canoe in the bay at Oak Island, Nova Scotia, noticed oak trees of a type that weren't supposed to grow in that part of the world. They looked more closely, and found a heavy iron ring from an old ship under one of the trees. Since then, thousands of people have figured the ring must be part of something bigger. In 1849, treasure hunters found bits of gold on the drills they were using, but they soon hit seawater and had to give up their search.

No one is sure who buried the treasure on Oak Island, or even what it is. For a while people believed it was the fortune of the pirate Captain Kidd, but it seems

Whoever put the treasure at Oak Island went to an awful lot of trouble. Excavations have revealed complicated tunnels and platforms built to protect it. But, so far, no one has been able to find the treasure itself, so it remains a mystery.

Kidd's treasure, if it exists, is buried somewhere in the South Pacific. Another theory is that the treasure belonged to Queen

Marie Antoinette, who sent a ship to hide her wealth in the New World before she was forced off the throne of France.

Faking It

Counterfeiting—making money from scratch—has a long and somewhat shady history. The earliest recorded forgery was in 540 B.C., when Polycrates of Samos used fake gold coins to pay a debt he owed to the city-state of Sparta. Centuries later, when the Bank of England opened for business, no one thought at first to make up special bank notes. Receipts for a customer's deposit were written on ordinary paper purchased from a stationer's shop. It didn't take the bank long to figure out that anyone could buy the same paper and write an official-looking receipt.

Some tobacco certificates (see above), once used for cash in the first American colonies during the 18th century, bore the notice "To Counterfeit is Death."

GOVERNMENTS DO IT TOO

Individuals aren't the only ones who counterfeit. Governments do it too, if they believe it's for a good cause. During World War II, the Nazi government of Germany tried to wreck the economy of England, its main enemy, by forcing imprisoned printers and engravers to make phony British £5 notes. The prisoners did such a good job that England had to withdraw all the £5 notes with the design that the prisoners had copied. To this day it is illegal for anyone, even a collector, to have that German counterfeit money. The Americans pulled a similar trick on the Japanese during the same war, printing fake Japanese money.

Artistic Crime

In a sense, a good counterfeiter is a true artist. Before France adopted euros, its money was printed on paper that one young Frenchwoman noticed was very similar in texture to ordinary airmail letter paper. So she used it as the canvas for her extremely accurate copies of French francs. Unlike most counterfeiters, who run their products off a printing press, this woman did each bank note by hand. Her talent with a brush was so great that she was successful in passing off her "paintings" as real money—for a while.

A Kenyan gentleman named Elias Mutumbe was so proud of his handiwork on a series of fake Kenyan pound notes that he wanted some credit for it. So instead of copying the portrait of his country's president, he put a picture of himself on the money! Needless to say, as soon as he tried to spend it, he was carted off to prison.

He's Been Framed!

J. S. G. Boggs says he is an artist, not a counterfeiter. In 1984, Boggs was doodling on a napkin while having a cup of coffee at a diner. He doodled a number "1" in each corner, then a floral frame around the edges; he made a note of a friend's phone number on one side with her name above it. He added a sketchy portrait in the middle and filled up the rest of the white space with scratchy marks, trying to get the extra ink off the pen's roller. When the waitress came over with his check, she said something like, "My, that looks like a one-dollar bill!" She said she'd take his artwork as payment for the .90¢ cup of coffee— and even gave him a dime in change!

So off he went, drawing fake money and offering it—as barter, he says—for restaurant meals and various goods. According to Boggs, his art isn't just the hand-drawn bank notes—it's the entire transaction. Boggs draws the money, then offers it in exchange, say, for a shirt. The shop owner accepts the deal, and gives him the shirt and a receipt. Then Boggs frames the whole sequence: the phony bill, the shirt, and the receipt—and that, he says, is the work of art. Museums and art galleries agree, and show his work.

Faking It Around the World

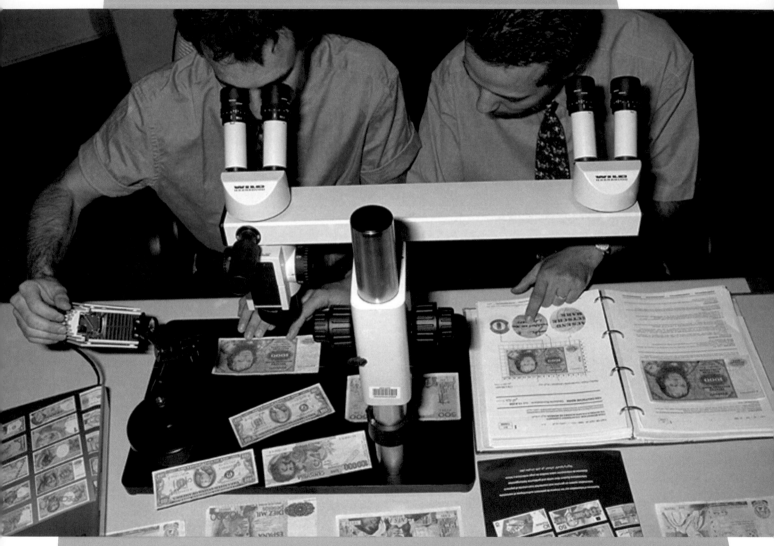

Workers at Interpol closely examine counterfeit money.

Because counterfeit money can cross borders so easily, counterfeiting is a serious international crime. The International Criminal Police Organization, better known as Interpol, was created in 1923 so that police in each country can get help from their colleagues in other countries when phony money is being made.

Nowadays Interpol also tracks down smugglers and criminals on the run, but its original job was to catch counterfeiters. It sends regular bulletins to police departments all over the world with examples of the latest known made-up money and news about where it is coming from.

Keeping It in the Family

Some families work together to make money. The Johnson family of Toronto did just that in the 1880s. Their family specialty was literally making money. Papa Johnson engraved counterfeit plates for bank notes, on which his daughters forged bank officials' signatures.

The Johnson sons printed the bogus notes, then Mama Johnson sold them to a wholesale money dealer. By the time the famous detective John Wilson Murray caught them, the Johnson family had put more than $1 million into circulation.

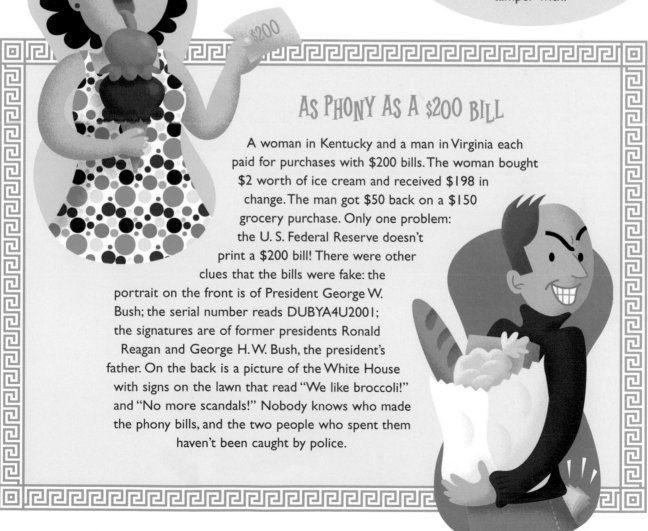

CHECK it out!

Counterfeiting currency goes back to when coins were invented. Someone figured out that they could be "clipped," have a tiny bit cut off—not enough so that anyone would notice, but enough to make new coins from the bits. Or a pile could be shaken in a leather bag until gold dust collected. It wasn't until 400 years ago that someone decided to cut a pattern around the edges of the coins to make them stronger and harder to tamper with.

AS PHONY AS A $200 BILL

A woman in Kentucky and a man in Virginia each paid for purchases with $200 bills. The woman bought $2 worth of ice cream and received $198 in change. The man got $50 back on a $150 grocery purchase. Only one problem: the U. S. Federal Reserve doesn't print a $200 bill! There were other clues that the bills were fake: the portrait on the front is of President George W. Bush; the serial number reads DUBYA4U2001; the signatures are of former presidents Ronald Reagan and George H. W. Bush, the president's father. On the back is a picture of the White House with signs on the lawn that read "We like broccoli!" and "No more scandals!" Nobody knows who made the phony bills, and the two people who spent them haven't been caught by police.

Arrested 38 years after the Great Train Robbery of 1963, Ronald Biggs is due for release in 2020.

Stealing It

Robbers sometimes argue that they have a higher purpose than just making themselves richer. For centuries, bandits known as *dacoits* terrified travelers in India, stealing money and murdering in honor of their goddess Kali. Perhaps the most famous robber of all time is Robin Hood, who has gone down in legend for "stealing from the rich to give to the poor."

Ronald Biggs, an Englishman, took part in one of the most famous robberies in history—the Great Train Robbery of 1963. A gang robbed a train, from Glasgow to London, of more than £2 million in bank notes (that's worth about £50 million today). Only £350,000 was recovered, and four of the 17 people involved (including Biggs) were never caught.

Biggs ran away to Brazil where the British police had no right to arrest him. He became a celebrity and something of a tourist attraction—famous rock stars on a visit would get their pictures taken with him.

But when he got sick in 2001, he decided he wanted to go home. So at the age of 75, he flew back to London—and was promptly arrested.

Computerized Catburglars

ATMs are almost robber-proof. There are a few tricks up thieves' sleeves, such as gluing the cash slot shut and then forcing it open after a customer has abandoned the transaction. But going to all that trouble usually doesn't pay off very big, so serious crooks don't bother.

The big scores are in bank fraud, or using the convenience of electronic banking to help yourself. No sooner had banks started to computerize, than dishonest people got to work on cracking codes. A young computer whiz illegally figured out the security codes at the large London bank he worked for and "withdrew" £9 million through the bank's computer system. He promptly left town, but he was so proud of his work that he left the bank a note: if they let him keep half the money, it said, he would let them know how he did it! The bank, eager to prevent such a crime from ever happening again, agreed to the deal and used the information to improve its security.

U. S. banks figure they lose as much as $12 billion a year to various frauds involving checks and ATMs. Most often, a thief will deposit a check to his bank account and make a withdrawal at the same time. Before the bank finds out the check is no good, the money taken out against it is long gone.

CHECK it out!

One New York bank robber thought he'd make his getaway by appealing to the greed of others. He threw money behind him as he ran, expecting people to ignore him and concentrate on picking up the cash. It didn't work. They ignored the cash and called the police to pick him up instead.

Unbreakable Banks

Montreal, Quebec, used to be the world capital of bank robberies. Twenty years ago, there were about 900 hold-ups there every year—and in half of them less than $2,000 was stolen. Nowadays, Montreal police respond to barely 100 robberies a year.

New technology has made banks into electronic fortresses. They are equipped with video cameras at the tellers' stations and the ATMs, so even if robbers get away, they're easy to recognize and catch later. There are alarm systems everywhere, and cash is kept in time-locked cash boxes—boxes that won't open until three or four minutes after the combination is punched in. Most robbers don't want to hang around the bank that long. And if for some reason they did stay, they wouldn't find much to steal: as customers use debit and credit cards more, and big and small companies use electronic direct deposits to pay their workers, banks keep less cash on hand than they used to. Considering that the penalty for a hold-up can run from ten years to life in prison, a few hundred dollars of loot hardly seems worth the risk.

Though you might have seen it done in the movies, breaking into a bank vault is next to impossible. Vaults are usually built with very thick concrete walls and reinforced steel bars. Space-age metals—so tough they will burn a drill trying to go through them—are mixed into the cement. The doors are made of reinforced steel and have computerized locks with secret codes. Sophisticated alarm systems go off immediately if they feel the heat of a dynamite stick, the banging of hammers and chisels, or the vibrations of a drill.

Protect Yourself

Credit and debit cards aren't just conveniences for honest bank customers, they can be goldmines for crooked ones. Thousands are stolen every day out of people's wallets or cars. And even if your cards are still present and accounted for, someone could be using your financial information for dishonest ends.

As we conduct more and more of our business over the telephone or the Internet, our numbers can be snatched out of thin air. This is known as "identity theft" and it's the fastest-growing kind of crime. The smart bandito has realized: why muss and fuss with nasty guns and getaway cars when you can sit at a computer keyboard and order piles of dough, diamond rings, airline tickets, and awesome threads at somebody else's expense?

How Identity Theft Works

• You sign a credit card receipt and leave a copy of it behind—with your account number right on it. A fraudster can trace that number back to your name, your name to a street address—and that's all the information he or she needs to order all sorts of goodies off the Internet.

• You hand over your credit card to pay for a meal. The waitress goes off with it and brings back your receipt to sign. Everything seems perfectly normal. What you don't know is that the waitress has a second job as a "skimmer:" she's rigged the scanner that reads your magstripe to make a copy of the information on it. And she plans to have second helpings with your unwitting help.

• You get junk mail that says you have been "pre-approved" for a new credit card. You don't want it so you throw it away. A dumpster diver finds it. Hello? Your unwanted credit card goes on a Caribbean cruise without you.

PLAYING IT SAFE

Here's what you need to know to protect yourself and your money from the less honest people out there.

Plastic Money

• *Know* what all your account numbers are and who to call in case of trouble, but keep this information in a safe place, separate from where you keep the cards.

• *Don't* lend your cards to anyone.

• *Don't* let someone take your card out of sight when you hand a card over for payment.

• *Get* your card back as soon as possible when using it to pay for something.

• *Don't* sign a blank receipt.

• *Never* leave your cards or receipts lying around.

• *Save* your receipts and reconcile your account statements as soon as they come in.

• *Immediately* let your bank know if there is any suspicious activity on your accounts. The sooner you report it, the sooner the bank will get word out to cease financial transactions using those numbers.

On the Internet

• *Always* use a secure browser.

• *Deal* with companies you know and trust.

• *Look* for security logos, digital certificates that allow you to check if the site is real, and privacy policies that assure you your personal information will not be shared.

• *Ask why* if the site asks for more than your name, address, e-mail address, and card number. Feel free to not answer questions you think go too far.

• *Print* a copy of your transaction confirmation and expect to get an e-mail confirming your purchase.

• *Be suspicious* about unsolicited offers from people and companies you don't know. If something sounds too good to be true, you can bet your bottom dollar that it is!

In the Mail

• *Tear up* financial junk mail before throwing it away.

• *Don't* give your personal information to anyone who asks for it.

PERSONAL ACCOUNT

SHRED-O-MATIC

Conning You Out of It

Can I interest you in…a tower? Apparently Count Lustig's offer was too tempting for two people to pass up. Each of the victims paid $50,000 to be the sole proud "owner" of the Paris landmark.

Con artists use their devious smarts and smooth-talking to scam many a person out of his money. In 1925, a sweet-talking Czech calling himself Count Victor Lustig persuaded two separate wealthy individuals to "buy" the Eiffel Tower from him. He said he had bought it from the French government because they needed the money but he didn't really want it.

The World Wide Web is a very exciting place, but when it comes to money it can also be dangerous. The amount of money lost to digital desperados has been nearly doubling every two years—from $3 million in 1999 to $6 million in 2001, with the average take from any one person increasing from $300 to $518 in the same period. The scams can be anything from offers for cheap Internet access, to phony business opportunities, to online auctions that don't send what you think you bought once they've got your credit or electronic debit payments.

Going Phishing

Schemers dangle all sorts of bait to hook unsuspecting victims. When an e-mail pops up asking you for information that gets too personal, chances are you're being "phished." Phishing is done by unscrupulous hackers who create e-mails and links to fake websites that look just like ones you already know.

"Sorry to bother you," the e-mail might read, "but our accounting department crashed and we lost all our client information. Could you send it again—your address, bank account number, debit number, your PIN…" The real businesses whose identities the phishers are "borrowing" say they would never ask their customers to send confidential information by e-mail. If you get a request like that, it's guaranteed to be from a dot.con artist.

The 411 on the 419

The most notorious cyber swindle is known as "The Nigerian Scam" or the "419 Fraud," from the country it has mostly been coming out of since the 1980s, and the section number of the Nigerian Criminal Code that prohibits it. It is number three on the hit parade of Top Ten Internet Frauds, and represents about 10% of all money stolen electronically.

The scam begins with a letter, fax, or e-mail addressed to you personally, telling you that a Very Important Person (VIP) in Nigeria needs your help. This VIP is in great danger, or needs to ship a large quantity of something valuable out of the country without the Bad Guys (BGs) knowing. Or the VIP has left you money in his will, or he's going to send you a Very Large Check (VLC) so you can buy something expensive for him.

Midas longed to be rich. When the god Silenus offered to make any wish of the Greek king's come true, Midas asked that everything he touch turn to gold. His wish turned out to be a curse: his food turned to solid gold when he picked it up, as did the drink in his cup. Midas prayed to the gods to take his wish away. They ordered him to bathe in a certain river to be returned to normal. Midas was rid of his wish, but from that day on, the river was full of gold.

But there's a catch. This VIP has to be absolutely sure he can count on you. So could you please

- Send money to help him escape and he'll repay you generously. Or
- Send money to get the shipment out of the country because if he does it, the BGs will know. (Oh, and you will be repaid very generously.) Or
- Send money to pay for the lawyers to get the VIPs will processed. Or
- Send small bills while waiting for the VLC to arrive.

If you go for it, another message arrives. The money you sent wasn't enough, or there have been "complications" or there's a tax that needs to be paid. So could you please send more money? And then more money… and more money…. Needless to say, your money's gone for good and you never see a penny of the riches you were promised.

Sadly, thousands of people have been caught up in this game. The average amount lost by any one person is over $5,000. The scam has netted an estimated $5 billion in ten years.

GETTING ON THE A-LIST

New York City busboy Abraham Abdallah liked to read—and dream. His favorite reading was the annual *Forbes* magazine list of the 400 richest people in the United States. He only earned $350 a month, but he wished he could be on that list. Well, if he couldn't be as Abraham Abdallah, he could be if his name was Oprah or Steven Spielberg or Martha Stewart. Using public documents, he found out the addresses, Social Security numbers, and account numbers of dozens of wealthy people. And with that information, he transferred a total of $22 million from their accounts to his own over a period of six months. He tripped up trying to transfer $10 million in one go, because the bank contacted the real account holder to double-check. When police caught him, he had a collection of 800 fake credit cards in lots of recognizable names, but not his own!

CHAPTER 7

WHERE MONEY GROWS

Planting the Seeds of Saving

hy not spend your money now? It's tempting, but it's also tempting to invest, when you see how your money can make you more money. Put in the right investment, like a savings account, your money really can grow like Jack's beanstalk.

There are many ways to invest your money. Your grandparents may have put money aside for you into a savings bond issued by the government. You can't touch it for whatever the "term" (the amount of time you are lending it to the government) is, but by the time it "matures" (is ready to cash in), it will have increased by 5% or 6%, or whatever the interest rate was when the bond was purchased. A lot of families find this a good way to save for university tuition.

Many people think the stock market is the best place to grow your money, and the market can be an exciting place. You'll get a backstage tour of it in this chapter. But it is also a very complicated place. Instead of trying to make a go of it on your own, you'd be better off pooling your money with other kids through an investment club at your school, or through an educational organization such as Junior Achievement.

This Little Piggy Went to the Stock Market

If you've ever traded collector cards, you have an idea of how the stock market works. If your friend has a card you want, you offer to trade one you have for the one you want. But if other people also want that card, your friend can say, "You'll have to give me two of your cards for that one of mine." Her card has doubled in value: what she paid for it is now worth two other cards originally bought at the same price.

When you do that with money instead, it's called investing. You don't buy cards, though. You become a shareholder, by buing a piece—called a share or stock—of a company. Say the company makes cellphones, and their product has been selling like ice cream on a hot day. The time has come to build a bigger factory and hire more people to make even more of The World's Best Cellphones (WBC Inc.).

If you give them some of your money, and a lot of other people do the same, then WBC can build and hire and make even bigger profits—and you have a right to part of those profits. If other people hear how well things are going for WBC Inc., they're going to want to own part of the company too. Since the company only issued 1,000 shares, and 2,000 more people want to buy them, then the one share you bought when they were first offered, you can sell for at least double what you paid for it.

Information is the key to good investing. In 1867, the stock ticker (below) was invented, which sent share prices out everywhere the telegraph could take them. Now ordinary people could know what was happening, and it opened the markets to more investors. The markets grew again once the Internet made it possible to research companies and exchange activities online.

CHECK it out!

If you want to be a millionaire, set aside five dollars a day for ten years. Then take that amount, invest it wisely in the stock market, and leave it alone for 40 years. You'll have at least $1,000,000. (Hey, nobody said it was going to be fast and easy.)

You Bet

So is the stock market any different from a casino? Yes, in a very important way. If you were to gamble on a casino game, the only way you'd have of knowing your chances of winning would be by calculating how often that game pays out. You don't get anything back for your money except the excitement of possibly winning.

If you put your money into a company, you own part of the company—plus the excitement. Before you decide if you want to invest your money, you can do research to lower the risk. Who runs the company? Do they know what they're doing? Do they have enough money to start their business and keep it going? Have they succeeded or failed at other businesses? If the company has a good track record, that's much more reliable and real than winning two or three times in a row at a casino. And if your investment turns sour because the people who run the company did something dishonest, then you can go after them to get your money back.

The stock market is the engine that drives the economy, making it possible for companies to grow and for individuals to increase their own wealth by contributing to that growth.

MIND OVER MARKET

The markets reflect the mood people are in. They feel that buying stocks is a risk worth taking when companies are producing lots of goods because there's demand, and hiring more people so there is less unemployment, and there is low inflation, meaning your money goes far to buy what you need. But if people are worried about their jobs, or think their money doesn't go as far to buy things and companies aren't making as much, they tend to sell their stocks and the markets fall. That's why the success or failure of the stock market depends as much on psychology as it does on plain facts and figures.

The Name Is Bond

Companies like WBC Inc. also borrow money from people and offer to pay it back, with interest for the trouble. That is called a *bond*—as in "my word is my bond." A company issues bonds when it knows it will be able to make enough money to return the loans. And the bond is backed by assets, things the company owns. So if WBC Inc. goes broke, bondholders will be the first to collect if there's money from the sale of WBC's buildings, computers, desks and whatever else it has. But, shareholders will only get the money that's left after that—if there is any.

WBC Inc. is asking you to take a gamble that they'll be able to sell thousands, or even millions, of their way cool pocket cellphones. And if they do, your bet will turn out to your advantage. And if they don't, you lose your money.

Governments issue bonds when they need cash but don't want to raise taxes.

Buy How about you? VICTORY BONDS

Stock Market Talk

The stock market is an exciting place where millions can be made and lost in seconds flat, or where a small investment, properly handled over many years, can turn into a significant sum. If you want an insider's glimpse into the world of trading, you can start by learning some of the colorful language.

The busy floor of the New York Stock Exchange.

Analyst a person who watches companies, and recommends to brokers and the public whether they should buy or sell.

Bear a grumpy animal that symbolizes the feeling that the stock market is going down; in a *bear* market, prices are falling; brokers and investors have a *bearish* attitude when things aren't looking good.

Bid the price at which you can sell a share or a bond.

Bond a loan to a company or a government.

Broker a person who finds stock buyers for stock sellers, and sellers for buyers.

Bubble a mania for buying certain shares that isn't based in reality, but in people's eagerness to buy. Bubbles always burst.

Bull a brave animal that symbolizes the feeling that the stock market is going up; in a *bull* market, prices are rising; brokers and investors have a *bullish* attitude when things are looking good.

Insane Indicators

Market indicators are employment and inflation numbers that provide clues about how the economy is doing. People tend to buy stocks when numbers are good, and sell when the numbers aren't. But some investors swear they can tell if the market is heading up or down according to the craziest things.

Thing to Watch	Market's going	Why	How accurate?
Aspirin® sales	down	If the economy is doing poorly, people get more headaches and buy more Aspirin®.	Not at all.
January effect	up or down	After calculating their taxes in December, investors buy and sell in January according to how well they've done. If they buy, the market's going to rise for the rest of the year; if they sell, it will fall.	Correct 46 times out of 52 since it was first noticed in 1950.
Lipstick sales	down	When women feel broke, they indulge only in small luxuries, such as lipstick.	Not at all.
Hemlines	up or down	If skirts are short, like they were in the 1920s and 1960s, prices will go up; if skirts are long, prices will go down.	True, looking back in time; no guarantee for the future.
Super Bowl	up or down	If the American Football Conference team wins, stocks will fall; if the National Football Conference team wins, they will rise.	Correct 29 out of 36 times, or 80%, so far.

Dividend payments made to shareholders out of a company's profit.

Equity the amount of money you have invested; it grows as your investments grow.

Exchange a marketplace for buying and selling shares.

Mutual Fund pooling your money with other people to be able to own a variety of stocks. A manager of the fund collects the money and buys different shares—you don't own stock in any one of those companies, but you own a share of the fund itself.

Portfolio the sum total of all the securities you own; a healthy portfolio should have a good mixture of companies' stocks and bonds and mutual funds.

Profit a company's earnings after it has paid its employees and all the costs of running the business; may be paid out to shareholders, or put back into the company.

Security another word for stock or bond.

Share when you own a company's *stock*, you are a *shareholder*. You own part of the company and you have a share in how well or badly the company does.

On the World Market

A Roman road, Via di Mercurio, at Pompeii.

How did the stock market come about? It depends on whom you ask. The Italians will tell you it started in Italy, the French that it started in France, the English that it started in London, and the Americans… well, you get the idea. What is sure is that as soon as people started trading, other people thought they could make some money on the deal.

Way back in Roman times, when citizens were asked to help pay for the building of roads, aqueducts, and monuments by lending money to the Empire, Romans got together and traded the receipts the government had given them for their loans. Why would they do that? Because if you were going to get your money back with interest from the government in a year but somebody was willing to give you cash for the debt right this minute for a little less, you might rather have the money now.

The same thing went on at fairs throughout Europe during the Middle Ages, when people who had letters saying they would get a shipment of wheat in six months were willing to trade the letters with someone who had a promise of 20 barrels of wine, betting wine would be worth more than wheat when the time came to collect.

Market Day

Historians agree that the city of Bruges in Belgium became the most important center of business in the 14th century. Traders came there with silk from China, spices from the East, carpets from Persia, swords from Damascus, wine from Italy, and wheat from France. With traders coming from all over, a family named Van der Beurs decided to open a hotel in the middle of town. To attract the traders, they hung up a sign showing three over-flowing bags of gold. Soon business was booming at the hotel, and traders and bankers knew that was the place to go to make money. The *bourse*, which is the French word for exchange, was born.

In London, traders had to find a new place to meet after they were thrown out of the Royal Exchange for being too rowdy. In 1698, one of those traders listed his office as being in "Jonathan's Coffee House." In the booming colony of Manhattan, Dutch and English traders met in coffee houses too, or just out in the street. The first organized stock market in America was called the Curb, because if you wanted to find a broker, you'd go outside on Wall Street.

But wherever the stock markets grew and whatever they were called, the word was out: trading stocks, bonds, and letters of credit was a way to get rich. And, it turned out, a way to go broke too.

The Paris Bourse in 1859. Women weren't allowed into the Paris stock exchange building until 1967.

TULIPS TO KISS YOUR MONEY GOOD-BYE

In Holland, people made and lost fortunes because of a humble flower. The tulip caused mass hysteria in 17th-century Amsterdam. No sooner did traders bring the first tulip bulbs to Holland from Turkey than everybody wanted some. In no time at all, some bright souls decided they could make more money trading the bulbs than planting them. So they started speculating that prices would go up, up, up. And tulipmania was on! At the height of the craze, one rare bulb sold for 4,600 gold florins (the price at that time of 20 tons of cheese), plus a carriage complete with two gray horses and a beautiful leather harness.

And then…it stopped. "Hey," somebody said, "these are flowers! You can't eat them, they go bad if you don't plant them. What were we thinking?" And prices just as quickly started to go down, down, down. People who had invested all their money in tulip bulbs suddenly found no one wanted to buy them any more, and what they owned was, well, something to be buried in the yard.

Crash Goes the Market

Panicked stock traders crowd the sidewalks outside the New York Stock Exchange on the day of the market crash, in 1929, known as Black Tuesday.

You might have heard of the Great Crash on Wall Street in 1929. The U. S. economy had been going gangbusters. There were ships being built, railroads running freight from one end of the continent to the other, farmers growing all that the country needed. From 1925 to 1929, the value of stock in the market went from $27 billion to $87 billion. Things were going so well that people were speculating instead of investing. Speculation is a form of investing that isn't about helping build companies but about gambling on whether prices for a certain stock or commodity will go up or down.

With so much speculation going on, the Federal Reserve, the country's central bank, started to worry that things might get out of hand. So they raised interest rates, making it more expensive to borrow money with which to invest.

When the supply of money got tighter, speculators got their cash out of the market. As prices fell, other investors worried about getting their money out on time. Panic spread, and in the rush to sell, the market lost 12% of its value in one day, a day that came to be known as Black Tuesday.

But Black Tuesday was not the worst crash ever. It was just the beginning of series of stock market disasters. The worst crash ever lasted two years, from 1930 to 1932. A thousand dollars invested in September, 1929, was worth $108.14 in July, 1932.

And the Moral of the Story Is...

The stock market crash happened a long time ago. Why should we care about it now? Because financial markets always go up and down. Though thousands of books, magazines, newspapers, and television shows analyze the market, no one's ever really figured out how it ticks or which way it's going to go.

In the 1980s, when people first started buying home computers and the possibilities of the Internet were causing great excitement, all sorts of companies started up promising to do all kinds of things, like deliver kitty litter right to your door or arrange a wedding with just a couple of clicks. Banks got so excited about this new way of doing business that they helped launch Initial Public Offerings (IPOs) on the stock market for staggering amounts of money before anybody knew if people really wanted to use the Internet, have their kitty litter delivered, or their wedding organized. (An IPO is the first time a company's stock is sold to the public. When a privately owned company has an IPO that means it becomes a publicly owned company.) The high-tech craze lasted until just a few years ago—and it turned out to be a bubble no different from Tulipmania.

AND IN THIS CORNER

In 1666, a Dutchman in America named Frederick Philipse got a bright idea. Since the local Native Americans accepted only wampum in exchange for the furs they trapped, the wampum itself could be made very valuable. Every time he got his hands on some, he buried it in huge barrels called hogsheads. Soon he had hidden so much wampum that when other settlers wanted some to buy goods from the Native people, they had to come to Philipse and pay whatever he asked for the wampum they needed. This little trick is called "cornering the market," and has been tried several times since.

HEY! I'M A MILLIONAIRE!

In the 18th century, a man named John Law was running France's financial affairs. With the royal family behind him, Law created the Mississippi Company, an enterprise meant to develop the riches of Louisiana, the French territory in America. People could buy shares in the company and be paid back when the sure-to-be-discovered wealth of Louisiana started rolling in.

The shares were wildly popular and demand kept growing. The more demand there was, the more the shares were worth, so buyers made a profit on their shares before a single acre in Louisiana was farmed or mined, because they could sell them to other buyers at a higher price than they had paid in the first place. The catch was that none of the money was ever put to use in Louisiana. It all stayed in France to pay off the government's debts and to make Law a wealthy man.

While the going was good, vast fortunes were made. Someone started calling the investors in the Mississippi Company "millionaires," a word that had never been used before. The word stuck around, but the money didn't. When people heard how their money was really being used, they sold their shares and values plummeted.

money myth

This lullaby was printed in a popular magazine in 1929:

"Oh hush thee, my babe, granny's bought some more shares
Daddy's gone to play with the bulls and bears
Mother's buying on tips and she simply can't lose
And baby shall have some expensive new shoes"

CHAPTER 8

SPENDING

MONEY

What's It Worth to You?

his is the fun part. But, believe it or not, it's not all that simple. Deciding what thing or toy or experience deserves *your* money takes some thought.

When you want to buy something, you have to meet the seller's price. Many things go into making up the right price: how rare or special the thing is, how difficult it is to make or find, how many other people want it, and how badly they want it.

The value of money itself changes over time. As people make more money and spend more money and the economy grows, it takes more of the same dollars or pounds or pesos to buy the same thing. The U. S. Bureau of Labor Statistics calculates that what you could buy for $1 in 1913 would have cost you $2.71 in 1955; $3.92 in 1970; $10.87 in 1985, and $17.89 in 2002.

Money is colorful stuff. It's colorful not only because of the glitter of gold, the sheen of silver, or the rainbow flecks on a bank note. There are lots of weird and wonderful stories about how it's spent—or not spent.

Money to Spend

About 300 years ago, the settlers and soldiers of Quebec were waiting for cash to come from France. Without coins, the soldiers of France who were fighting the English in the New World couldn't be paid. But Europe seemed to have forgotten the people across the Atlantic and had become quite unreliable about sending them any money.

The head of the garrison, Intendant Jacques de Meulles, knew he had to give the soldiers something. The soldiers needed money to buy food and drink, but there were simply no coins to be had. So the Intendant took a pack of playing cards and asked the soldiers and townspeople to bring him their packs too. On the back of each card he wrote 15 sous, 40 sous, or four francs. Then he signed each card, and the treasurer affixed his seal. Each soldier was given his pay in hearts, spades, diamonds, or clubs. With it he could go to the store and buy what he needed.

When the king of France found out what had happened, he was furious. Only coins issued by the government, he said, could be used as money. He demanded that the cards be destroyed. But people wouldn't give up their card money until the king shipped enough coins to New France to trade for the playing cards.

Over the next 60 years, the government of France kept forgetting to send coins to Quebec. Whenever a ship failed to arrive, the people remembered de Meulles's card trick and revived the habit of trading playing cards instead of coins (see below). In 1711, diamonds and hearts were worth 50 livres and spades and clubs were worth 100. When they ran out of cards, they used plain pieces of cardboard.

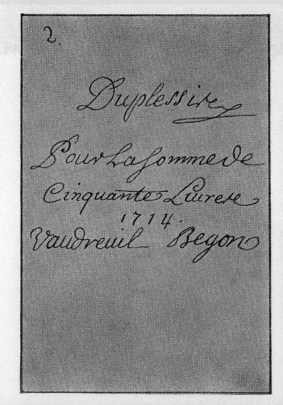

The Money's in the Mail

Cash was in short supply when the U. S. Civil War broke out in 1861. The North and the South both printed their own bank notes (each side refusing to accept the other's), but that didn't help the situation when small change was needed. Stores sometimes made their own metal tokens to give customers as change, but they couldn't be used at other stores.

Finally someone came up with a smart solution: why not use postage stamps instead of coins? The stamps were official, they had denominations printed on them— one, two, or ten cents—and everybody needs stamps at one time or another. People liked the idea, and soon everyone was going to the store to buy a loaf of bread or a bag of flour and paying for it with stamps or getting stamps as change from bank notes.

The front of the stamp case was transparent so people could see how much the stamp inside it was worth. The back was solid metal.

This great idea had one flaw. Stamps are meant to be used just once on a letter or postcard. Being passed from hand to hand, like coins, they began to fall apart. Yankee ingenuity came to the rescue. A certain Mr. J. Gault patented his idea of putting the stamps in tiny metal cases to protect them from wear and tear. Smart merchants soon began to put the names of their stores and businesses on the back of the cases, so every time someone spent one of the coins, they got free advertising.

SPENDING (KHAKI) GREEN BACKS

Soldiers at war are often cut off from the sources of the cash they need to buy what they need to live. Lord Robert Baden-Powell (who created the Boy Scouts) found himself in that situation during the Boer War in South Africa at the end of the 19th century. He was at a place called Mafeking when the money ran out. The soldiers there had been especially brave, using for a weapon a makeshift cannon nicknamed the Wolf. When Baden-Powell decided to pay the soldiers with money he issued himself, he drew a picture of the Wolf and had it printed on ordinary paper.

Even then, there wasn't enough of Baden-Powell's money to go around. When things got really bad, the soldiers ripped their khaki shirts into pieces and signed them over as "money" to spend.

Getting It

Before you can think about spending your money, you have to, well, earn some. How do you go about doing that? Well, you could write a fabulous book with a wonderful hero like J. K. Rowling, whose Harry Potter stories have earned her hundreds of millions of pounds, making her richer than the queen of England.

Or you could become a movie star. The actor Jackie Coogan was only six years old in 1920 when he made $1 million for starring in a movie called *The Kid*. He still holds the record for being the highest paid child actor of all time (that $1 million would be worth $8.3 million today). Child actors today are very lucky to get $1 million. MacCauley Culkin was paid between $1 and $2 million for *Home Alone*, one of the most successful films of all time. Haley Joel Osment, from *The Sixth Sense*, gets paid the same for his roles, as do Darryl Sorbera and Alexa Vega for the *Spy Kids* movies. The highest paid child actor of our time is Frankie Muniz, who is famous for his TV role in *Malcolm in the Middle*. He got a full $2 million for his role in *Agent Cody Banks*.

If you don't see yourself starring on the big screen, you could make lots of money by making something that everyone wants. Levi Strauss was only 20 years old when he left Germany for San Francisco in 1850, at the height of the gold rush, with tons of canvas to sell to the miners for tents.

But the miners didn't want tents, they wanted pants that wouldn't tear. So he made pants out of the canvas. When those proved too itchy, he found another canvas-like cotton material called *serge de Nîmes* (say it out loud) and created *denim* blue jeans.

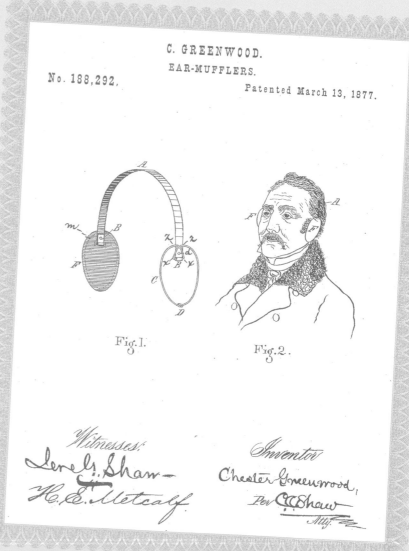

C. GREENWOOD.
EAR-MUFFLERS.

No. 188,292.

Patented March 13, 1877.

Fig.1.

Fig.2.

Witnesses:
Levere G. Shaw
H. E. Metcalf

Inventor
Chester Greenwood,
Per C. C. Shaw
Atty.

Inventing something really useful is another way to get rich. Chester Greenwood of Maine was 15 when he patented the idea of putting a metal headband between wool ear covers. He made a fortune selling the Greenwood Ear Protectors™ to the U. S. Army during World War I.

WORKING FOR YOUR MONEY

Thinking up ways to earn money is one of the prime preoccupations of human beings. Coming up with clever new ways to do it is known as "enterprise," a way of contributing to the world and a great outlet for your creativity. Here are some ordinary but useful things people you know might pay you for.

Babysitting: You can find out if your local school or community center runs a babysitting registry. Taking a course in babysitting safety is always a good idea, and can connect you to potential clients.

Seasonal chores: Mowing the lawn, raking leaves, or shoveling snow, for example.

Car wash: Set yourself and some friends up in your driveway with buckets, soap, sponges, a hose, and drying cloths. Waxing is way extra.

Dog walking: Bring lots of bags to poop-and-scoop.

Yard sale: Help your parents clean out the house. Make a deal to keep whatever money you get for your old books, toys, and clothes.

Locker-cleaning: Help your friends out when they can no longer deal with the spilling-out books, smelly sneaks, and empty chip bags.

Homework help: If you're really good at math or geography, show someone who's not how it's done, for a price.

Online searches: Put your computer wizardry to good use for someone who needs a lot of research for a paper or a project.

Be crafty: Decorate your friends' school binders with sparkles and stickers; make jewelry out of beads; weave friendship bracelets with bright silk yarn; buy old picture frames and jazz them up with seashells and sequins.

Enter: Science fairs, spelling bees, musical competitions. Essay-writing contests often have generous scholarships for prizes.

For What It's Worth

Buying clothing with the coolest logo or a game just because all your friends have one is fun, but not always the best use of money. The *price* of something is not always its *value*.

A lock of your hair isn't worth very much to anybody, except maybe your mother. But on an Internet auction site you can buy five strands of dyed black hair supposedly from a famous pop star's head for $50.

Price is determined by how many people want something at a certain moment and how much they are willing to spend. Value is what it means to you, today and tomorrow, no matter how much or how little it costs in cash.

That's why you can sometimes find today's gotta-have thingamawhosit on sale for 50% off six months after the buzz for it has passed.

Learning to wait for something—to see if you still want it after your first excitement about it, or to give you a chance to see if you can find it cheaper at another store or online—is an important part of figuring out how to handle your money.

GOING FOR A SONG

Have a listen to the price of music over nearly a century, from the days when people gathered around a piano in the parlor to sing, to the age of the Internet.

Format	No. of songs	date	price
sheet music	1	1920s	25 cents
45 rpm record	2	1950s	98 cents
album, vinyl	12 (average)	1970s	$3–$5
album, tape cassette	12 (average)	1980s	$8
album, CD	12 (average)	1990s	$15
MP3 download	1	2000s	99 cents

All prices are what the items would have cost at the time.

CHECK it out!

1.2 billion people around the world live on less than $1 a day.

Sometimes what you want is a whole lot more than your allowance or earnings will cover. For example, that really awesome mountain bike you saw at the store costs $250. If you could put $2.50 in a jar every week, you would have enough to own that bike in about one year and 10 months. It might seem like forever when you're just starting out, but watching your savings pile up towards a dream can be an amazing experience. Still, it's okay if you decide that it's just *too* forever. Then you can re-do the math: find a bike that's more your financial speed—that is, cheaper.

Have you ever wondered how good you are with money? According to an old English rhyme, you can tell by looking at how your shoes wear down:

Wear at the toe, spend as you go.
Wear at the side, be a rich bride.
Wear at the heel, spend a good deal.
Wear on the ball, live to spend all.

WORTH THEIR WEIGHT IN RUBIES

Just about everybody wears shoes and most of them are nothing special. You can pay more to have a famous athlete's name on your running shoe, or a really cool design. But once shoes have been worn, chances are nobody else is going to want to buy them. That is, unless you're looking at a pair of small, sequined red slip-ons with stubby high heels.

The Ruby Slippers are a pair of tiny, shiny shoes worn by Judy Garland as Dorothy in the movie *The Wizard of Oz*. The slippers in the original story by L. Frank Baum were actually described as silver, but because the film *The Wizard of Oz* was being made in color, it was decided to go brighter and bolder.

When the movie was shot, in 1939, the costume department of MGM studios made seven pairs, in case a heel broke, a shoe was lost, or a pair was needed on another set. For years, the shoes lay around the costume department at MGM. Then, in 1970, MGM decided to get rid of old costumes, and an employee found four pairs. Since then, the Ruby Slippers have walked way up the price ladder. One pair is on display at the Smithsonian Institution in Washington D. C. and is considered priceless. But in 2000, another pair fetched a price of $660,000 at an auction in New York.

Piles of Spending Money

Between World War I and World War II, the government of Germany couldn't pay its debts. No one trusted the money, so it was worth less and less. In 1922, what you could buy with a single Canadian dollar in Canada would cost 18,000 German marks. The government kept printing money in bigger and bigger denominations as prices kept going up and up.

During the 1920s, a man in a German restaurant ordered a cup of coffee. The menu said a cup of coffee cost 5,000 marks. The man drank it, called for his bill and saw he was being charged 8,000 marks. The price of a cup of coffee had gone up 3,000 marks, or 60%, in one hour!

The situation caused great hardships for the people of Germany. A single egg cost 100 million marks. A

By 1924, the German people shook their heads in amazement when they were handed 100 milliarden (that translates to 100 billion) mark notes.

wealthy man who had bought a life insurance policy in 1903 and paid his premiums for 20 years cashed it in and found all it would buy was a loaf of bread.

Workers would show up at factories on payday carrying laundry baskets and pushing wheelbarrows to collect their wages. They would dash to the stores to spend their money as soon as they got it, for fear that prices would go up. Eventually people lost all faith in the currency and began trading cigarettes, liquor, even hairpins and soap for food and shelter.

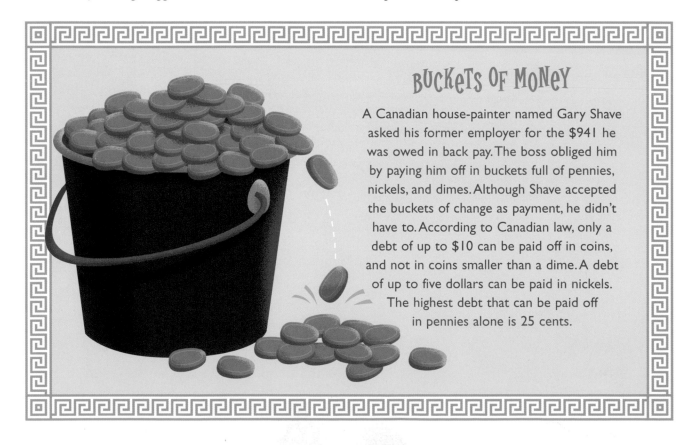

BUCKETS OF MONEY

A Canadian house-painter named Gary Shave asked his former employer for the $941 he was owed in back pay. The boss obliged him by paying him off in buckets full of pennies, nickels, and dimes. Although Shave accepted the buckets of change as payment, he didn't have to. According to Canadian law, only a debt of up to $10 can be paid off in coins, and not in coins smaller than a dime. A debt of up to five dollars can be paid in nickels. The highest debt that can be paid off in pennies alone is 25 cents.

CHECK it out!

Money is important and powerful stuff, but there are things money can't do. It can't make the sun shine on a rainy day. It can't keep you company when you're feeling alone. And it can't make somebody love you.

Try Spending This!

The German one-billion-mark and one-trillion-mark notes printed in the 1920s are not the highest denominations ever created. That honor goes to the government of Hungary, which in 1946 issued a bank note worth 100 quintillion pengoes (see below). A hundred quintillion looks like this:

100,000,000,000,000,000,000.

SPENDING ON YOUR CONSCIENCE

Reportedly, the American government occasionally receives money from citizens who feel guilty about something. A woman who re-used two postage stamps eased her conscience by mailing in 44 cents to cover the cost of cheating the post office. A man sent in $2,000 to settle a debt he thought he had with "the tax department and God"—but nobody knew what he was talking about. A government worker who had used office machines to photocopy private letters mailed in $20, four times as much as he thought he owed because "the Bible says to repay fourfold."

The Future of Money

Does money have a future? You bet. As long as someone has something someone else wants, there will always be money in one form or another.

For decades people whose business it is to look into the future have said that one day—soon, very soon, maybe even next week or next year—we will live in a cashless society. But it still hasn't happened and, chances are, it never will.

Why? Because as technology blazes its way into tomorrow, we find ourselves trying to balance convenience and privacy. It's great to be able to buy an expensive keyboard in a flash by swiping a card or punching in some numbers, but do we always want to leave a digital trail of who we are, what we do, and what we buy? As long as we want to keep some things to ourselves, we will always need cash. Cash is nameless and, once out of our fingers, invisible. It is quick, convenient, and forgettable—just the thing for keeping life simple.

If there were no criminals in the world, it would be a very different place. We wouldn't have armies of engineers working on ways to make our debit cards and credit cards as fraud-proof as possible. In the not-too-far-off future, we will have pictures taken of the unique pattern of the irises of our eyes or DNA samples of our saliva in a file somewhere, and every time we want to make a purchase we'll have to blink at a camera by an ATM or spit in a cup at a store, just to prove that we are who we say we are. But will the bad guys be right behind, trying to steal our eyeballs and our spit?

It's pretty sure that cool inventions that seem right out of a spy action film will keep on coming. How about a little bug juice on your bucks? Scientists have created a new kind of ink made from proteins found in a certain bacteria. If you dye a bank note purple with this ink and then shine a green light on it, it will change to yellow. You'll need a blue light to turn it back to purple. And if you try to scan the bank note, the bug ink will change color under the photographic flash of the scanner, and you'll wind up with a perfect copy of the bill, except it might be cockroach brown or fire ant red.

And someone's figured out that every magstripe has a unique sound. So when a credit or debit card is made, the issuer will record its own little song, and if anyone tries to tamper with it or make a fake copy, it won't sound right. Credit cards that only work when they recognize their owners' voices and password could soon become another weapon in the fight against fraud.

```
BRIAN JONES
1 Megatronic Gift
$539.95
PURCHASE & I.D.
CONFIRMED
```

AMAZING AND STRANGE

The way money looks and even sounds in the future may be different but not too different. There are already holograms on U. S. dollar bills, but not one of George Washington winking. Yet.

The countries of Europe have already taken a step towards an international currency—the euro—while the rest of the world clings to its rials and rupees and rubles. But as nations do more and more trade with one another, the speed and security of digital transactions make national currencies irrelevant.

The idea of money isn't likely to change. Money, whether in the form of coins, bank notes, checks, plastic cards, or computerized codes, is still an idea, not a thing. Who knows what people will accept as money in the future? It might be something brand new that we can't even imagine. Or it could be something old, like beads or feathers or cocoa beans.

One thing's for sure: your great-great-great-grandchildren will probably find the coins you have in your pocket today amazing and strange. As amazing and strange as you find gigantic stones, bricks of tea, or the ancient custom of trading elephants for groceries.

Acknowledgments

I owe a debt of gratitude to several people who added much more than their 2 cents worth to this book:

Sheba Meland, who really knows how to compound interest;
Anne Shone, who polished the manuscript until it shines like a newly minted penny;
Dave Cobbett, of MacDougall, MacDougall and MacTier, who took stock of my need for information;
Lona Freemantle, Principal, Pape Avenue Public School, who sets the gold standard;
Walter Macnee, president of Mastercharge Canada, who deserves full credit for his vision;
Jack, who has invested heavily in me, and Thalia, who is my fortune.

Photo Credits

For reasons of space, the following abbreviations have been used:

NCC: National Currency Collection, Currency Museum, Bank of Canada, photography Gord Carter, Ottawa.
SI/NNC: Smithsonian Institution, NNC, Douglas Mudd.

Page 7: NCC; 10: Charles O'Rear/CORBIS/MAGMA; 11 (top): SI/NNC; 11 (bottom): Minnesota Historical
Society; 12: SI/NNC; 13: U.S. National Archives; 16: William Taufic/CORBIS/MAGMA; 17 (top): SI/NNC;
17 (bottom): NCC; 18 (top): Richard T. Nowitz/CORBIS/MAGMA; 18 (bottom): SI/NNC; 19: SI/NNC;
20: courtesy U.S. Bureau of Engraving & Printing; 21: Guildhall Library, Corporation of London; 24: NCC;
25: courtesy The Louisbourg Marine Museum; 26, 27: courtesy U.S. Mint; 28: NCC; 29: courtesy U.S. Mint;
30: Robert Berdan/© Bank of Canada—used and altered with permission; 31: CORBIS/MAGMA;
32: courtesy U.S. Bureau of Engraving & Printing; 33: SI/NNC; 34: Charles O'Rear/CORBIS/MAGMA;
38: Haruyoshi Yamaguchi/CORBIS/MAGMA; 39: SI/NNC; 40: courtesy Municipal Archives of Amsterdam;
41: courtesy Federal Reserve Bank of San Francisco; 42: Guildhall Library, Corporation of London;
44: courtesy Federal Reserve Bank of San Francisco; 45: Guildhall Library, Corporation of London;
46: CORBIS/MAGMA; 52: Andrew Brookes/CORBIS/MAGMA; 60: Missouri State Archives;
61 (top): Guildhall Library, Corporation of London; 61 (bottom): Buisson, A./National Archives of Canada/
PA-014532; 62: courtesy Federal Reserve Bank of San Francisco; 64: ©Interpol;
66: MANCHETE/CORBIS SYGMA/MAGMA; 67: Bill Ross/CORBIS/MAGMA; 70: CORBIS/MAGMA;
74: Alan Schein photography/CORBIS/MAGMA; 75: Glenbow Archives NA-3338-1;
76: Alan Schein Photography/CORBIS/MAGMA—used with permission of the New York Stock Exchange;
78: Mimmo Jodice/CORBIS/MAGMA; 79: Hulton-Deutsch Collection/CORBIS/MAGMA; 80: Bettmann/
CORBIS/MAGMA; 84: NCC; 85: SI/NNC; 86: courtesy U.S. Patent and Trademark Office;
89: MGM/The Kobal Collection; 90, 91: SI/NNC.

Index

Page numbers in italics refer to illustrations.